THE
ENGLISH COUNTRY
HOME

THE ENGLISH COUNTRY HOME

Edited by
VANESSA BERRIDGE

Salem House Publishers
Topsfield, Massachusetts

PUBLISHED IN ASSOCIATION WITH

CONTENTS

HALF-TITLE PAGE *The hall at Spye Park in Wiltshire, a converted eighteenth-century stable block.*

FRONTISPIECE *Tumbling greenery and pots of pink pelargoniums in the porch of Dulverton Cottage.*

LEFT *A corner of the living room in part of an Irish castle imaginatively transformed into a family home.*

CONTENTS

RIGHT *The painted
recessed desk in the
drawing room at
Mount River displays
a colourful collection of
ornaments.*

ABOVE *The window
seat in Jilly Cooper's
kitchen is much
favoured by the
family's dogs and cats.*

FOREWORD

This book is about houses. It is also about the people who live in them and who turn them from mere bricks and mortar into homes. It is a celebration of a great and historic tradition which continues to the present day – that of the English country house.

Few countries have a finer heritage of domestic architecture, for the English have always identified with the land in which they were born and with the people who lived and worked there. Our houses reflect this: English manors frequently have more in common with the cottages by which they are surrounded than with houses of similar size elsewhere. This lent an air of cosy domesticity, grace and charm to the big house and tenants' cottages alike. Rambling gardens completed the picture, always designed with the modest scale of the houses in mind.

Innately English, too, is the desire to return to the countryside – and it was this longing that was the starting point for both this book and *Country Homes and Interiors*, the monthly magazine which is the source of the stories and photographs here.

You may ask, why now? Isn't it all rather nostalgic and irrelevant? Nostalgic, certainly, but irrelevant it is not. The more mechanistic our lives become, the more we yearn nostalgically for those virtues of serenity and beauty which are represented by our landscape and our houses. This book captures that nostalgia.

It is people who make houses and gardens come alive as an expression of their own personalities. Indeed, it is a fascination with the lives of others that makes their homes so intriguing; every house, garden or conversion featured here is seen through the eyes of the owners.

The English house appears in all its many guises – from a stately Norfolk manor house to a cosy and intimate Gloucestershire farmhouse that is a young family's second home. One chapter is devoted entirely to conversions; this, perhaps, is even more creative than designing from scratch. It must be enormously satisfying to turn a triumphal arch, a barn or a Quaker meeting house into a home, while maintaining a sense of the building's original purpose.

Many of our gardens seem to bear witness to that great gardener, Gertrude Jekyll; for example Long Barn, first garden of Vita Sackville-West, who later achieved so much at Sissinghurst. Each garden has its own tale. Most haunting is that of The Priory garden at Kemerton, planned by Peter Healing while a prisoner of war.

Inseparable from our houses is the landscape by which they are surrounded, for, almost without exception, it seems to inform the style and architecture of what is built there. The weathered yellow stone of Cotswold houses is a perfect complement to the rolling yet wild hills among which they find themselves. Much of our countryside remains miraculously unspoilt, as a walk round the Isle of Purbeck or along the Pennine Way will show. A chapter is devoted to these lovely and undiscovered corners of Britain.

English city dwellers dream of moving to the country when they retire, if not before. And most of us who have these dreams feel a twinge of envy for those who are able to live and work away from big towns and cities. Many of the lucky ones here are writers, including Jilly Cooper, Rachel Billington, Jeffrey Archer and Auberon and Teresa Waugh. Others have made the country work for them, such as the Evetts who furnish houses for the Landmark Trust.

This book is truly representative of the English country house in all its diversity. We have broadened our horizons from time to time, showing houses in Scotland, Ireland, in Wales, and even in Tuscany, but there is a common thread – these are homes created by English taste, which in itself has been formed by a landscape and culture of which Scotland, Ireland and Wales are an essential and inextricable part.

Vanessa Berridge, 1987

OPPOSITE *Corinthian columns frame the hallway at Carolside, a stately Border Country mansion.*

6

COUNTRY HOMES

An Englishman's home is his castle, so the old saying goes. And how true it is. The beauty of English domestic architecture has played an important part over the centuries in moulding the national consciousness, and indeed we must have some of the finest private houses of any country in the world. We choose to relax in our homes, for, unlike our European counterparts, we have no tradition of eating out or of promenading up and down the boulevards on a Sunday afternoon. Far more people own houses in England than in, say, West Germany, a much wealthier country.

We are all of us fascinated by other people's houses and find it hard to resist the temptation to peer through the lighted window opening on to the street of a country town. For a house is like a diary – infinitely revealing of its owner's secrets. The building itself and its position – enclosed in a village or exposed in rolling countryside – are both clues to the owner's character, as are the arrangement of the pictures and furniture and the choice of wallpapers and fabrics.

The houses featured here are all markedly individual – all bear the imprint of their owners and are greatly loved and cared for. They are as intimate as memoirs – and the chance to visit them unheralded and unnoticed, yet as an old family friend, must be irresistible.

OPPOSITE *Above the drawing room at Spye Park*
runs a wide gallery hung with exquisite
Victorian tapestry fabric.

WOOD HALL

Amanda Evans

Photographs by Peter Rauter

*Presiding over the
sunny yellow kitchen
is a statue of Hermes,
discovered in a corner
of the garage.*

Supposing you had grown up in a city knowing that one day you would inherit a rambling country mansion, you would at least have had time to prepare mentally for country life – snowed-in winters, huge heating bills and the quiet.

Annabel and Brian Charlesworth had no such leisurely preparation. Ten years ago they lived in the heart of London and thought vaguely of moving out in to the country one day. Then an elderly cousin whom they had never met died suddenly, leaving them an enormous house in East Anglia. The Charlesworths did not stop to ask whether it was the sort of house they would have chosen, or even whether they wanted to settle in East Anglia. They simply put their London house on the market and moved in.

Decoration was a problem. 'We didn't move into an empty house like most people, and decorate from room to room. We moved into a house crammed with old paintings, furniture and ornaments. It was all dark and dreary, but faintly picturesque – and I was quite undaunted,' laughs Annabel. She admits now that she was a little naïve, but says it is only rarely that she thinks, 'If only I'd known then . . .'

Annabel has done it all the hard way. 'I believe that when it comes to decorating, you have to make your own mistakes. It's the only way to learn.' Ten years later, she is still decorating; not with an all-consuming passion, but with sporadic inspiration. She continues to discover treasures – porcelain buckets, glass jugs, earthenware pots. As a result, there is no particular theme in the house. 'It has just evolved.' Many of the rooms have been left just as they were found. In others, Annabel simply drew on her newly acquired source of furniture and ornaments to create a different atmosphere in existing rooms. And she is still shifting things about to create new corners. Where rooms have been redone, she has blended the new look with the old, so that nothing seems out of place.

The canopy for the bed in the main bedroom was made by using some spare curtain poles and antique tassles.

A few new touches brought the large sombre entrance hall to life. The dark oak panels were stripped to reveal a paler colour, and Annabel livened the other dark colours with a fabric in red, blue and gold stripes, and bought a huge, sagging sofa to go in front of the blazing fire – a welcoming sight for returning sportsmen.

Annabel found the mock-Adam drawing room rather precious and decided to tone it down. She chose bold flower print curtains and painted the walls a neutral colour, picking out the plasterwork in related tones. Kelim-covered tables provide more warm shades and a tapestry chair, commissioned from a local craftsman, completes the lavish effect.

Another local man made their kitchen in just one week. It is a vast and jolly yellow place, with plenty of room for the children and their hobbies – and for cooking. Dogs amble round, flop and snore in front of the stove, all presided over by a statue of Hermes.

He was found, says Annabel, in a corner of the garage and they 'didn't know where else to put him'. Bits and pieces found around the house are dotted along the windowsills, with extra finds that Annabel has not been able to resist. 'I've bought so much junk, which is ridiculous when the house is full of it, but it just seems to absorb everything and it's difficult to know when to stop.'

The main bedroom is decorated in gentle, dusky colours that complement the well-worn Aubusson carpet. Annabel sponged the walls seven times to achieve the right shade. She put a pretty canopy over the bed, which she raised so that she and her husband can look out of the window.

Annabel finds the house a source of constant pleasure. She is currently creating a sports room. A collection of old leather cases, hatboxes, gun cases and leather boots give it a special atmosphere and on the walls hang sporting photographs of past generations of Charlesworths.

When the family moved in, the garden, complete with Victorian glasshouses, box hedges and 100-year-old yew trees, was 'beautiful, but crumbling'. Annabel aims to restore it to its former glory – and make it a much more manageable proposition for herself and a one-day-a-week gardener.

The joy of Wood Hall is that even though it had an established character of its own it has been flexible enough to accommodate many fresh ideas. The Charlesworths have not obliterated the old style, but added new layers, rearranged things and brightened it all up. Consequently it never looks like a house in the throes of decoration, but remains a comfortable and welcoming home, whatever Annabel is doing. Which is just as well, because she is still dreaming up new projects.

ABOVE *The comfortable mock-Adam style drawing room.*
OPPOSITE *The enormous bathroom was created by knocking two rooms together.*

DENE HOUSE

Elizabeth Dickson

Photographs by
Fritz von der Schulenburg

Behind Dene House lies a field where, amid clucking poultry and wild daisies, a vast tree trunk wallows like a whale in shallows of long grass. The tree was Helen's birthday present last year, conveyed to its resting place by two cranes and a truck. It is also a good example of the Kimes' special gift: their knack of absorbing the past, and giving old things a new life in the present.

Robert Kime is an antiques dealer; his shop is in a converted outbuilding a few steps from the house, past the sprawling *Clematis alpina* and through the vegetable garden. His wife Helen writes bestselling children's books (under the name of Helen Nicoll) and runs a company producing cassette readings of classic novels. At first she used the kitchen table as a desk, but now she has expanded into an enviable office, a white room under the eaves approached from an outside staircase. A home life has been gradually established whereby both husband and wife run their separate businesses without getting in each other's – or the family's – way.

When the Kimes bought their eighteenth-century West Country home, Dene House, which is thought to have been built as the dower house for the local manor, it had been empty for years. The man who lived here in the 1920s had used it as a summer residence, and left a legacy of soft fruit beds, tennis lawn and a boxroom piled with mouldering tennis balls. As for the roof, 'we could stand in the cellar and see the stars', Robert recalls.

Nineteenth-century tiles were made into a new roof and a handsome stone porch found locally replaced a modest wooden one. From the front of the one-room-deep house, an Edwardian extension is just discernible. The whole building integrates extremely subtly with the surrounding garden.

A statue of Orpheus under the trees by the short front drive stands on a carpet of speckled fritillaries, and along the garden wall a pleached lime hedge is in the early stages of growth, with a catmint border

planted below. There is a corner for shade-loving plants such as Solomon's seal, lilies of the valley and hellebores. Delicate blue granny bonnets harmonize with the natural architecture of shrubs and in early summer the wisteria cascades from boughs reaching to the upper windows.

Nearly derelict when they found it, 'the house was overgrown', explains Helen. 'I had the romantic ideal we all have about the pre-war way of life: lentil soup, chickens in the garden, not an alternative lifestyle and not a grand style either. My mother was a great cook and her love was expressed through feeding – she welcomed people with offerings of food.' To begin with, Helen followed her mother's example, feeling she had to provide even mere acquaintances with slices of newly baked bread. But nowadays, even when the children are home from school and friends are staying, Helen says her dedication to enter-taining is not what it used to be. And how has she achieved this liberation from the stove? 'Simply by keeping less in the larder.'

With its dresser, Irish vegetable table, geraniums on the windowsill, flagstone floor and comfortable old sofa in front of the fire, the Dene House kitchen still has an atmos-phere of bounty about it; indeed, it is the central point of the home. But despite its atmosphere of rustic leisure, the house itself has been reorganized to become a highly practical place. The kitchen, for instance, which was once the drawing room, leads through to a convenient pantry and utility room where most of the modern appliances can hum away together. Off this is a conserva-tory, which in turn takes you to the garden. The new drawing room is across the hall – an escape from the activities elsewhere, de-corated in quiet tones of grey-blue, butter-milk and faded reds.

Upstairs are the main bedroom, two guest bedrooms and two bathrooms. A few steps up are the attics, taller now that they have been opened up to follow the shape of the new roof. These are the children's quarters. 'Rooms do change,' observes Robert who, with his wife, is constantly trying pictures and furniture in new positions. At present all their shell pic-tures (a collection of sailors' valentines) have been recalled from their various positions to be amassed in one room. A stable of horse pictures has been regrouped on a landing.

Above the stove in the kitchen hangs a framed sepia photograph of Yatesbury Stud dray horses, sited exactly so that it can be seen from the kitchen table, where friends

LEFT *Robert and Helen Kime in their picturesque courtyard garden.*

LEFT *A tumble-down eighteenth-century barn at right angles to the back of the house has been converted into a conservatory.*

OPPOSITE *Lloyd-loom chairs, Moroccan painted glass lamps and a host of resident climbers including a plumbago and a passion flower fill the conservatory.*

and family gather for meals and conversation. It depicts the horses sturdily lined up, the power to pull coaches up the hill on the old Bath Road.

As the family grows, so rooms are adapted. Yet the general principle that has been followed from the start is putting right what is owned already, rather than buying things new. It is the impression of belongings weathered by time, of textures gradually overlaid. Old flower chintz curtains acquired from a country house sale were re-made. Linens may be well used, but they are finely sewn and soft, and chair materials are home dyed to the right shade rather than discarded. True, the bath is new, but the Edwardian mahogany surrounding it was once the panelling in a local bank. The windows in the conservatory are Gothic, with painted glass from a David Hicks sale; placed as they are now in walls of old brick, you might think they have been the source of light here for decades. Yet until recently it was a disused barn.

All this is an indication of the Kime approach to restoration. They abhor the 'clean sweep' mentality, where the modifications of different eras are ruthlessly swept away in search of an earlier 'authentic' look.

'When a house is built, it is as if a clock has been wound up, and you can't stop it. You can, of course, put it back to an earlier time, if you do it sensitively enough, but it's easier – and usually better – to let the clock run on. We've adapted Dene House slowly, thinking carefully before adding new elements and cherishing all that's been done before.' Their motto could perhaps be 'if it isn't broken don't mend it'.

Helping the Kimes with their conversion of Dene House was Mary Lou Arscott, an architect friend, and a gifted carpenter, Morris Hopkins. The house is now alive again and perhaps entering its golden era. The ghost, a soldier from the Boer War, may visit occasionally; even when he does this is a place to feel at peace in, well settled, part of a continuum. As Helen comments: 'It is a kind house.' Robert adds: 'And it works.'

The spacious kitchen (RIGHT) was originally the drawing room; a spare bedroom (BELOW) is home for a splendid half-tester bed.

THE RING

Charles Darwent

Photographs by Timothy Beddow

Betty Hanley corrected me twice – in the nicest possible way – during my tour of her house in Essex: the first time when I pronounced her birthplace *Mitch*egan ('It's "*Mish*egan" – you English never say it right'); the second when, peering myopically into a Regency birdcage, I expressed my swinish admiration for what I called 'a pair of bone birdfeeders'. 'Oh, those . . .' said Miss Hanley, with a devastating lack of affectation, 'they're ivory . . . ah . . . they're Ming, actually.'

Silence.

This gives some sense of the well-bred, Henry Jamesian charm that characterizes both Betty Hanley and her house, The Ring. The Jamesian quality is more than just coincidental. Amid that great emigration of patrician Americans, Betty Hanley, her mother and her aunt all fled Kalamazoo for Europe in the Twenties. Her aunt, Fern Bedaux, bought the Château de Candé in France and among their friends and fellow émigrés was one Wallis Warfield Simpson. It was on the terrace at Candé that the famous wedding photographs of the Duke and Duchess of Windsor were taken.

'I grew up with lovely things at Candé,' remarks Betty, and The Ring is testament to this legacy. The shade of Aunt Fern is very much present: tangibly in the gargantuan Louis Vuitton trunks in the bedrooms upstairs, and intangibly in the elegance with which her niece has decorated her house. Nor (Americans being a democratic people) is Mrs Bedaux's the only spiritual presence at The Ring: she shares it with an actual ghost, the small son of a gamekeeper, who got a splinter of yew in his finger and died of lockjaw sometime before the last war.

The family of this small unfortunate were the last full-time occupants of The Ring before Betty Hanley found it, twenty-four years ago. It was in an unhappy state. Built as a Gothic menagerie in 1776, the house stands in an arboretum planted on the remains of a Saxon fort: hence its name. The Ring had been a focal point for the local gentry who wished to picnic to the chirrupings of exotic birds, and by 1962 trees were growing out of what had once been the roof. Betty took a year to convince the owner that she really did want the house, and slightly less than that to finish it – including felling forty trees, connecting mains water (although the house still relies on a generator for electricity) and raising the level of the moss-covered roof by several feet. 'It was,' she says (a monster of understatement), 'such fun.'

In all of this, Betty was enthusiastically assisted by friends like the late John Fowler, of Colefax and Fowler (who recommended the dragged *trompe l'oeil* panelling in the dining room), and writer on country homes, John Cornforth, who provided expert advice on Gothic restoration. Although she used the

house's Gothic origins as the dominant motif in her designs, Betty was careful to avoid obvious over-restoration. 'After all,' she reasons, 'if the whole house is reproduction, then the original features get lost.' Moreover, she says 'the house protested' if she tried to 'make it too grand'. The final effect is formal without being stuffy, a country house on a cottage scale.

The garden is a case in point. Here, the trappings of a great estate are reproduced in miniature – guinea fowl instead of peacocks; two rows of apple trees instead of an avenue of elm or oak; a small, white, symmetrically sited summerhouse instead of an Adam temple. To deepen the perspective, Betty Hanley has Gerry the gardener cut the grass short in the middle of the garden, but progressively longer as the eye moves away gradually from the central axis.

As with everything else at The Ring, formality is tempered with intimacy: under a lilac bush to the right is a wooden cross with the name 'Hyram' painted on it – Betty's late lamented dachshund. ('Gerry put that up,' she says, touched; then, smiling quizzically, 'I'm not sure you're really allowed to have crosses for dogs.')

Nevertheless, canine company (named Cleo and Sheba) still inhabits The Ring in voluble profusion, the Hanley family being rounded off with an omnipresent, scornful and snoring cat. 'The house was built as a menagerie,' remarks Betty wryly, 'and some things haven't changed.' With that ineffably feline sense of self, the cat poses in front of the dining room fire on one of the six Gothic chairs copied by furniture restorer Peter Boswell from the chapel of a stately home; the fireplace is also a copy from the chapel, although one which is contemporary with the house. The dogs, meanwhile, content themselves in the drawing room with Empire chairs from Betty's mother's house in France. These were originally gilded, now they are washed white. Mrs Hanley would not have minded: she, too, was a dog-lover – although, confesses her daughter, in forty years her French never progressed beyond 'Jacomo! (her chauffeur) Où sont les leashes des dogs?'

'It's just such a mixture,' says Betty, having to raise her voice over the sonorous snores of the cat. It is. Cheek-by-jowl in the drawing room are precious wooden French madonnas and delightful (but undistinguished) bucolic English wooden birds; wildly valuable Chinese parchment boxes and an ordinary Victorian barley-sugar-legged table,

painted mint green. 'I used to buy junk furniture and do it up,' says Betty, typically self-effacing. Among the 'junk' which she bought was a then unfashionable Victorian marble bust of a country girl, now in the corridor outside Betty's bathroom; friends who thought her mad at the time now ogle it covetously and regret their former prejudice.

These same friends are put up in some style at The Ring. Beyond the cottage kitchen (which contains a large brick fireplace with a collection of mysterious brass boots on the chimneypiece) and the herb garden is a guest annexe, with its own entrance under a profusion of wisteria. Here again the décor is eclectic, the motif canine: Chinese temple dogs peer up maliciously at dogs on tapestries; embroidered dogs grimace at dogs in oils, ink dogs smile archly at dogs in porcelain. One of the porcelain dogs has fairly colourful origins: Betty points at it, sitting on the windowsill of the orange en-suite bathroom, and says vaguely, 'They're used by Norwegian ladies of … ah … a certain profession: they turn the dogs to face the window when they're free and away from it when they're … ah … occupied.' Blessedly few Norwegians ever wander past Betty's house.

Guests relegated to an inside bedroom are hardly less fortunate. One is a tent in Brunschwig wallpaper (copied from an early American chintz), with that delightful air of a secret place under the eaves – a sensation heightened by Aunt Fern's Louis-Vuitton trunks and a pile of Nat King Cole records on the floor. The other is a more delicate and beautifully symmetrical room, with a central casement window looking down the path of apple trees to the summerhouse.

Once more, Betty's designer's eye is evident: wooden curtain rails are painted to her own design by an artist friend, the casement is outlined in a strong, French border print.

And, as one might expect, Betty's own bedroom is that same pleasing contrast of the precious and the homely: exquisite seventeenth-century French floral prints, ingeniously fixed to the sloping walls; a profusion of antique lace and linen (and two sleeping dogs) on the bed; and finally a mysterious tin of a proprietary substance called 'Not On The Floor'.

'I think,' says Betty, grimly indicating the dormant forms, 'you can imagine why.' Heedless, the dogs sleep on.

A feature of the spare bedroom is the central casement window outlined in a French border print.

Empire chairs and loose-covered furniture create a mixture of period and colour in the drawing room.

PAGES 24–5
Gothic windows in the dining room are flanked by trompe l'oeil *panelling, an inspired idea of the late John Fowler, who assisted in the interior renovations.*

CAROLSIDE
Jackie Cole
Photographs by Hugh Palmer

True to the best romantic fiction, Hugh and Sarah Poole-Warren fell in love with a photograph. The picture was of Carolside, a faded Georgian mansion in a wooded valley in the Scottish Borders. They bought it on impulse. Hugh was working as a landscape gardener in Hampshire at the time, and they were living happily in an architect-designed modern house near Basingstoke.

'We saw an advertisement for Carolside and fell in love with it,' recalls Sarah. 'It wouldn't have mattered where it was; it was just what we had always dreamt of.' Within ten days it was theirs and Sarah, having always lived in the south of England, found herself preparing to move north. It took three days to move the entire Poole-Warren household of three dogs, three horses, a cat and two children the 400 miles from Hampshire to the Borders, a trip Hugh and Sarah won't forget.

'Hugh took the Range Rover with three horses, the Great Dane, the Labrador, the cat and the quiet child in tow, while I followed up the MI with the noisy child and the excitable dog.'

They moved in on 5 January during a snowstorm, when their idyllic vision had taken on a more realistic shape. 'It was sleeting, there was no heating and the solid fuel cooker had gone out,' recalls Sarah. Unpacking with icy hands caused many breakages. But despite the cold, the whole family was captivated by Carolside. Hugh

had always been on the move; it was the first time that he felt he had roots, so aware was he of the history of the house.

Carolside was built in the 1740s on the site of an early sixteenth-century peel (watch) tower. Later alterations added touches of grandeur to the house – two wings were built in the early nineteenth century, pillars put up in the hallway and a splendid Connemara marble fireplace was imported from an Irish mansion. Sadly, though, the house had been affected by the property developments of the Seventies. The estate was divided into lots and the house sold separately to an architect, with just fifty acres. When Hugh and Sarah bought it in 1980 for £110,000, it desperately needed renovating. The interior had fallen

prey to a glut of brown paint and wood-chip wallpaper, those hallmarks of the Seventies, and the fireplaces had been filled in.

Undeterred, Hugh and Sarah set about restoring the house to its former glory. The sheer size and scale of the rooms was daunting, in terms of both time and expense. Hugh did all the painting and decorating himself, while Sarah made up the curtains. Cost was a major consideration, as the windows were both many and large. They skilfully adapted an eighteenth-century design for the drawing room, using acres of cheap fabric, lined and interlined for extra weight and then lavishly trimmed with a heavy fringe. Fortunately, most of the furniture from Hampshire went well in this Georgian house. Faced, however,

ABOVE *The grand Corinthian columns in the hall were a later addition to the early eighteenth-century house.*

with a dramatic increase in wall space, they frantically collected paintings and prints.

The garden proved to be almost as much of a challenge as the house. The five acres of formal gardens, which had been laid out by Lady Gilmore, a previous owner and keen gardener, were now very overgrown. With the help of a retired gardener who had worked at Carolside during the time of the Gilmores, Hugh was able to salvage many of the precious old roses and shrubs. Apart from a walled kitchen garden, the remaining forty-five acres are mainly woodland and were used as a deer park until the 1930s. Deer still occasionally come down across the gardens to drink in the River Leader Water, a tributary of the Tweed, which cuts across the lawns in front of the house.

As often happens in romantic fiction, this story has a happy ending. Thanks to the experience of restoring Carolside, Hugh and Sarah have built up a thriving interior decorating service, together with Brian Dunlop, making up curtains in the basement of the house and selling fabrics from a small shop. They have recently opened an office in newly developed Ransome's Dock in London and now decorate houses all over the country.

DULVERTON COTTAGE

Jackie Cole

Photographs by Timothy Beddow

To the casual passer-by, Dulverton Cottage seems all a country cottage should be, with heavy thatch, thick cob walls the colour of clotted cream and uninterrupted views across a wooded valley to the Exmoor hills. But rural Britain stops at the front door. There is nothing cottagy about the style, nothing chintzy about the furnishings, cream teas are not on the menu and the atmosphere is not so much cosy as liable to give a nervous visitor the creeps.

James Reeve was born in Devon and then lived and worked in London as an artist before returning to Somerset to paint. He has lived at Dulverton Cottage for some years: just long enough to be accepted by the locals and time enough to stamp his style on the house. He is a great traveller and inveterate collector: stuffed and preserved snakes, birds, shells and eggs, picked and gathered from as far afield as Guatemala, the Yemen and the Australian outback, are now arranged on tabletops and windowsills. 'I don't think you ever reach saturation point in a cottage like this. I will always be adding bits and pieces'.

Not too surprisingly, Dulverton Cottage is a listed building: its oldest part, a former tannery, dates back to the fourteenth century. When James bought the house it was sadly dilapidated and badly needed re-thatching – a task of enormous proportions as the house consists of three cottages knocked into one and is therefore over sixty feet long. Another major job that James felt was a top priority when he first moved in was to block up the window at the front of the house which

opened at street level on to the main road: 'Interesting as the local ankles are, I couldn't see myself making a lifelong study of them.' Now all the windows on the ground floor are at the back of the house and face out over the garden – on balance, a more picturesque scene, James feels.

The kitchen had to be almost totally rebuilt. A wall was knocked down between the kitchen and the dining room and a local carpenter made cupboards which James then scumbled off-white to match the walls. James adores both cooking and eating and, in preference to a conventional stove, he has installed a huge catering stove that copes admirably with extravagant and simple meals alike. Just inside the kitchen door, a boa constrictor lies curled up waiting to give visitors its own particular welcome. A collection of pottery jugs adorns the windowsill above the sink and the evidence of James's travels even extends to here, in the form of a rather surreal statue from South America.

In contrast to the creams and pinks of the rest of the house, the downstairs drawing room is painted a deep blackberry colour. The room has a relaxing, yet mysterious, feel to it: faded leather sofas, Turkey carpets and souvenirs ('including a monkey's hand from the Amazon jungle that grew hairs after it had been put in its glass ball') all add to the atmosphere. Dulverton Cottage is full of surprises and, indeed, occasionally the grotesque.

A room upstairs has been converted into a second sitting room but it is only used in

LEFT *An impressive wooden beam rescued from a mill in Exeter divides the kitchen, with its huge catering stove and butler's sink, from the dining room.*

RIGHT *A fantastic piece of coral brought back from Madagascar makes a background to a collection of Haitian sea urchins and natural sponges.*

FAR RIGHT *A collection of stuffed, preserved and carved snakes formed during James Reeve's many trips all over the world.*

OPPOSITE *On the walls of the main bedroom in the oldest part of the cottage are the remains of a beautiful fifteenth-century painted frieze.*

ABOVE *The drawing room is filled with magnificent furniture and curios.*

ABOVE RIGHT *James Reeve in his studio which, in complete contrast to the rest of the cottage, is sparsely furnished.*

BELOW *A fine old oak settle and patchwork quilt lend a homely air to the dining room.*

summer when the wisteria frames the window. Like the kitchen beneath it, this room is Georgian (the newest part of the house) and James tries to ensure that the decorations are in keeping with the period: even new acquisitions somehow look as if they have been here forever. James's bedroom and adjoining bathroom are in the oldest part of the cottage (fourteenth century): the bedroom is suitably furnished with period oak furniture. A huge bed which belonged to James's grandparents dominates the room, the head upholstered in fading antique embroidered tapestry. On the walls are the remains of a fifteenth-century frieze: at one time, it was thought to be French because of its fleur-de-lys pattern, but it has now been attributed to a travelling English artist. In the true tradition of old houses, Dulverton Cottage has its ghosts: one of the bedrooms is said to be haunted by an Elizabethan woman and there is, supposedly, an Edwardian croquet player in the garden.

James spends most of his day in the studio, which is sparsely furnished and very obviously a place in which to work. When James is not painting, he spends as much time as possible in the garden. Clematis, jasmine and roses climb over the porch and an avenue of limes leads down to a period arched gate opening on to an area James has nicknamed the mausoleum. He would like to be buried there apparently. Now covered in climbers it looks – like everything else at Dulverton Cottage – strange but somehow right.

MOUNT RIVER

Sally Phipps

Photographs by Ianthe Ruthven

Like the Brenta Canal near Venice, the various branches of the Dublin Canal pass through town, country and raw industrial landscape, and now and then on the borders appears a house that is like an oasis from the past. Mount River, standing at some distance from Dublin, is one of these: its outstanding architectural quality lies in its utter simplicity and serene proportions without and within. Calm, compact and modest as a beached seashell, it takes its name from its position on a small hill and dates from the 1740s. Anglo-Irish literature abounds in houses with huge windy drawing rooms, miles of passages and flying staircases, but a house of such sane and gentle scale as Mount River is seldom mentioned. And anybody who lives in one is usually grateful for the fact.

In some respects it is halfway between a classical mansion and a cottage. The basic plan of the house is two rooms deep on either side of a central stairwell. The formal front is a delightful blend of classical motifs, including (the experts say) a small Gibbsian doorway and a floating pediment with a miniature Diocletian (half-moon) window. Originally rendered and whitewashed, the rendering has been patched up over the years, giving a patina to the graceful façade. The builder was clearly someone of considerable means; he would have been known as a yeoman farmer in England or a squireen in Ireland.

The present owners of Mount River, Oliver and Sarah Wendell, have brought to the restoration of the house a spirit of understanding and celebration. They worked with the architect John O'Connell, who is becoming to Irish houses what John Fowler was to English ones: many have benefited from his keen appreciation of individual atmosphere and history.

A semicircle of lawn reaching to the doorstep means traffic is now banished from the front of the house; you enter from the back door by way of a charming stable yard and what must be the prettiest basement in the country. It is painted a dark yellow with much red in it, the sort of colour often found on exterior walls in Italy, combined with woodwork of an almost black green.

The kitchen, which has been moved to the first floor, is presided over by a large and comforting stove and opens on to the library. Although entirely different worlds, the two flow together, linked by harmoniously squared proportions and occasional decorative cross-references. Both rooms contain round tables with graceful French-print tablecloths that drop to the floor, and each is painted a slightly differing tone of cloudy yellow which absorbs the changing light from tall windows and alters with it.

The library, which sometimes doubles as the dining room, is a particularly pleasing room. Unusually beautiful castellated library bookcases in oak are split to frame the

ABOVE *The drawing room has glowing red walls which give an impression of faded lacquer, and a beautiful eighteenth-century French carved stone fireplace.*

LEFT *The cloudy yellow and dark green kitchen opens directly on to the library on the first floor.*

OPPOSITE *The library also doubles as the dining room; the chairs are Regency, the bookcase Gothic revival and the paintings Napoleonic.*

kitchen door and run along the gable wall. Filled with a catholic collection of volumes, they date from the Gothic revival of 1810 and still retain their original brass screens. A fine eighteenth-century walnut bow-fronted chest stands between the two windows which overlook water and distant mountains. Keeping the Irish weather at bay are generous tent-like curtains of hand-blocked French cretonne in a yellow and pink floral design.

For all its elegance and all its treasures (including a sophisticated art collection and numerous valuable pieces of furniture), this house is small-scale and mellow and easy to live in. Sofas and stools are jumped upon by children and dogs, and rugs from country house auctions are thrown over the bracken-coloured matting which runs throughout.

The drawing room, across the hall from the library, is essentially a night room. Though it has references to the library, in its almost identical eighteenth-century carved French stone chimneypiece and its curtains of a similar but more ornate print, it is very dark in daytime. At night, the red walls glow by lamplight and the paint gives a shadowy impression of faded lacquer. Some of the architectural details are Irish: the simple arches over the door and desk recess; the light yet robust joinery of the squared ceiling architrave, chair rail and door panelling; the tall, delicately barred windows. But the muted colouring, the richly painted inset lacquer desk and the mixture of modern and old paintings are sophisticated and Continental. Visual jokes crop up all over the house: on one of the drawing room tables the bust of a brash punk figure gazes unseeingly at a magnificent antique Chinese bowl.

Such idiosyncratic touches as this wittily contradict the main theme – of restored calm and elegance. The mixing of the house's serenity with other things, including some of the harsh, even ugly, elements of the modern age, is interesting and lively. And because the restoration has been done with such complete assurance, nothing jars.

Paintings, drawings and watercolours hang throughout. The core of the collection, which includes many Irish works, is contemporary, but it takes in eighteenth- and nineteenth-century pictures, a charming little collection of Napoleonic portraits as well as works by David Tindle, Martin Gale, Michael Healy and Sean O'Sullivan. Perhaps the most charming piece is the landscape over the fireplace in the drawing room.

The owners' interest in painting is reflected

in the colour schemes, which are almost like the work of a watercolourist themselves. The paintwork was devised by interior decorator Laura Jeffries, who built up its delicate tones and cloudy luminous effects with a system of glazes. The result is as natural and changeable as light itself, with the colours subtly graded on the woodwork. The warm Italian shades that grace the downstairs rooms give way to gentle birds'-egg colours in the hall and upper regions of the house. The flowing sense of space within the small scale of the proportions of the lower and upper halls and stairway is accentuated by the marvellous 'wateriness' of the colouring.

Against this background the robust simplicity of the staircase and woodwork are thrown into relief. This whole area is lit by just three windows – one of the smaller floor-level windows of the top storey, an arched mid-stairway window and the graceful fanlight over the front door. Taken together, they demonstrate the variety and harmony that Georgian windows lend to the inside as well as the outside of a building.

Divided by the upper hall, the two spacious bedrooms also have windows to the floor, low concave ceilings and delicately hand-painted wallpapers. Behind them are two bathrooms and a small bedroom overlooking the stable yard. The view of the yard with its stone buildings, cobbles and slates in a slanted pattern is as delightful, in its way, as the front view of rolling countryside.

The former *haygard*, or farmyard, has now been transformed into a miniature walled garden. Tons of topsoil have been imported and old walls made good. The flowers and trees are growing vigorously, nurtured by gardener Jack Walsh, brought out of retirement for the job. Complete with rustic summerhouse and a lime walk, this new garden harmoniously pays homage to the original spirit of the house.

SPYE PARK

Caroline Phillips

Photographs by
Peter Woloszynski

This is the story of the Spicers of Spye Park, and if they sound like characters from an eerie film, there certainly has been plenty of attention paid to the sets.

Spye Park – so-called because of its unique vantage point over the village of Lacock in Wiltshire – was originally a Jacobean house lived in by a Mr Baynton, who gambled it away.

Major John Spicer, great-grandfather of the present owner, then moved in, demolished Mr Baynton's house and built a Victorian stately home on the site. This in its turn was largely destroyed by fire in 1974, and what remained turned out to be riddled with dry rot. So the Spicers decided to move 200 yards – to live in the stables. 'Stables are much more manageable than half a house – which is all that was left of our old one,' reckons Rosamund Spicer with realism.

A long drive leads up to the converted stable that is now Spye Park, home for the Spicers and their children – Edward and Louisa (John lives in a lodge on the estate). The façade and yard were virtually untouched during the conversion, though three new windows were added. The rich Cotswold stone has a lovely weathered quality that contrasts pleasingly with the clean white shuttering.

The interior, however, needed more attention, given the fact that the library had been a loose box and the main bedroom a hayloft. Deathwatch beetle and structural weaknesses had to be attacked, too, and the odd wall moved a bit. 'We tried not to convert it too much,' says Mrs Spicer. Yet the overall effect – despite a profusion of horse prints – is more stately home than stable. As for the furnishings, fixtures and fittings, 'That's a short story,' says Mrs Spicer, 'we just tried to bring everything we had.' 'Everything' included fireplaces, doors and the family coach. A few things, designed for a vast Victorian house, proved too large; luckily, many fitted.

One coup was the placing of the magnificent carved double doors from the old drawing room. These were put in front of the carriage washing area, now the entrance hall. The doors open on to a flagstoned hall and bare stone walls. Their raw quality is juxtaposed with refined Hepplewhite chairs, a seventeenth-century blanket chest and delicate paintings. This is indeed a house of contrasts.

The drawing room houses many more heirlooms. It was originally a coach house, and the brick floor has been kept. Panelling was brought from the house to create a superb gallery, used as another sitting room. The

gallery is wide – 'We didn't want it to seem like the top of a double-decker bus' – and has its own set of windows. This creates a light and spacious feeling emphasized by the pink walls and the white ceiling with its massive beams. Photos and pictures abound, with the family in sepia on one side of the fire and watercolours and prints of the house on the other. The grandeur of scale is softened by lots of cushions and inviting sofas.

In the library next door are a marble fireplace and arched french windows that lead on to the terrace. The main feature of this room is the exposed vertical timber of the old stabling, which gives a warm glow, heightened by dark furniture and drapes in golds and yellows. By contrast the atmosphere in the dining room is rich and splendid, with a claret-coloured carpet, burgundy wall hangings and plum-covered chairs, embroidered with the family crest ('a hand throwing a petrol bomb,' says Mr Spicer). Embroidered Victorian hangings are covered with horse pictures. Mrs Spicer explains, 'when we came to the house, every picture had a horse in it.'

After this, the kitchen, romantic and rustic, comes as a complete surprise. It is the blacksmith's forge converted, complete with original stacked furnace (though an oven has

been added). 'When we first saw it, the room was black,' recalls Mrs Spicer. 'We put in skylights and exposed all the original surfaces.'

There are five bedrooms. In the main bedroom, a massive canopied bed, made by Mr Spicer's grandfather, has been built in. 'And the drapes are old curtains that came from the house – next winter I might actually get round to finishing them,' adds Mrs Spicer. The magnificent ochre canopy perfectly complements the heavy beams, and the room is prettified with delicate furniture and floral curtains. All the bedrooms are attractive and rural, and each has a canopied or four-poster bed. In Edward's room Mrs Spicer confides, 'the insurance people say this bed is Tudor so I've hammered it securely to the wall to hold it up'.

Like so many of the other intriguing features in the house, that is just the sort of down-to-earth touch one might expect when people move from a stately home to a stable.

BELOW *A collection of suitcases, riding whips, ivory brushes and hunting prints in the downstairs cloakroom.*

RIGHT *The kitchen was originally the forge.*

CERNEY WICK FARMHOUSE

Josa Keyes

Photographs by Tom Leighton

When John and Jan Gayner first saw Cerney Wick Farmhouse it was appallingly dirty, very shabby and overrun with students. But they loved it immediately, and now, several years later, Jan claims; 'It is still my favourite place in the world.'

John is a London doctor, so the Gloucester-shire farmhouse is the Gayners' second home, where they spend some weekends and where Jan lives in the school holidays with their sons Justin and Toby. In London Jan feels torn by all sorts of pressures: in the country she finds that she can relax and enjoy being with the children. One feels she slightly resents time given to adults.

The house is built of grey Cotswold stone, its heavy stone roof tiles green with moss. Farmland stretches away on all sides, and the view is studded with the flooded gravel pits so characteristic of the Thames valley. To one side of the house a barn has been converted into a family games room, with a large rug on the floor, and an indoor tennis game set up for rainy days. Later, when the boys are older, it will be ideal for parties.

A lovely antique quilt bought in Covent Garden market in London covers a dilapidated chesterfield. Jan Gayner spent many hours removing several layers of paint to reveal the golden wood of the shutters.

ABOVE RIGHT *Blue-and-white gravy drainers taken from meat dishes decorate the walls of the downstairs cloakroom.*

The house itself is long and low, and filled with Jan's treasures. She cannot resist markets and junk shops, and once had a sign in the back of her car saying *Caution, I brake at antique shops.* She really does not like anything new, and thinks clothes are a complete waste of money; whereas buying 'clut', as her boys call it, is a true passion. The price and place of purchase of every plate, tray-cloth, sampler and biscuit box is engraved on her memory. 'If it's under a tenner, I'll have it,' she swears. The only problem is where to put it all, so things dangle from the ceiling in

attractive baskets, to the consternation of guests, who are constantly banging their heads. Jan's favourite markets include Covent Garden on Mondays, Bermondsey, and Brick Lane very early on Sunday mornings. She subscribes to an antiques gazette which gives notice of auctions throughout the country. One morning in London, she saw that a ten-foot dresser base was being sold at the right price in Marlborough. It was just what she had waited four years to find to complete the kitchen, so she raced down the motorway and arrived just in time to snap it

up. It now occupies one wall in the kitchen, adorned with a stuffed carp and a metal duck.

Jan's particular method of decorating calls for years of accumulation, as she waits patiently for the right components to turn up. The downstairs cloakroom demonstrates the method perfectly. Having bought the original lavatory bowl – blue-and-white china with a pattern of ruined temples – Jan could not find a drainage pipe to fit. She appealed to Doulton in Cirencester, who kindly took the bowl to the potteries to see if they could find something suitable. On the way back there was a car crash and the bowl was broken. Where could Jan find another? By a stroke of luck, an identical bowl turned up in Bath a month later.

The cloakroom walls are painted a streaky sunshine yellow and hung with blue-and-white gravy drainers taken from meat dishes. The blue and white basin is fitted with early taps, while the mahogany wooden surrounds came from various junk yards and the lavatory seat from Bermondsey market – that it fitted was more by luck than judgement. The room took four years to complete – but triumphantly vindicates the method.

Wood is Jan's favourite material, and gloss paint her least. Furniture, fireplaces, steps and panelling have all known the rough kiss of paint remover. Jan claims that, pregnant with Toby, she was found by one of the workmen in tears, clutching a bottle of gin, as she tried to get the paint off the last step. 'I can't go on,' she wailed, 'there are sixteen coats!' 'You can,' he said, and she did.

Sharp green is the dominant colour of the house, and goes well with all the bare wood. Upstairs, some of the bedroom furniture came from the nursery on which J. M. Barrie modelled the one in *Peter Pan*. Walls and ceilings are papered in small, cottage prints and finished with friezes. Beds and furniture are strewn with cushions covered in antique tray-cloths.

The children have the attic to themselves, and the garden is fairly rough – lending itself happily to their games. Our visit is cut short by lunch, and a projected expedition to the cinema. Jan, her duty to adults done, returns with relief to the needs of her family.

The house might only be a second home, but it has given Jan a joyful excuse to unleash herself – 'like a dervish' – in pursuit of furniture and ornament.

In the farmhouse kitchen old shutters have been skilfully used to make cupboard doors.

COUNTRY GARDENS

Gardens are as personal as the houses they surround – the personality of those who tend them is as surely revealed by their choice of plants and trees as it is by their selection of lamps and carpets.

The loveliest and most successful gardens are those which are designed with the age and style of their house in mind, and where the garden becomes an extension, a natural adjunct which enhances the beauty of the house, cottage – or mansion. The creative partnership of the architect Edwin Lutyens and the great gardener Gertrude Jekyll proved this over and over again wherever they worked – and it is true of the gardens illustrated on the following pages.

Gertrude Jekyll's influence can certainly be seen in the bright beds of colour at Clifton Hampden, The Priory and Jenkyn Place. She also left her mark on the creator of Sissinghurst, Vita Sackville-West, whose Kent garden is a place of pilgrimage for enthusiast and amateur alike. Vita's first garden, created with her husband, Harold Nicolson, was at Long Barn, some miles from her later, more famous home, and her work there is beautifully described by Jane Brown.

Different prospects open up for us at Chidmere and Minterne Magna, and all make us aware that gardening is as crucial to the English way of life as caring for and decorating our homes.

OPPOSITE *Long Barn in Kent, where Vita
Sackville-West first revealed her gardening
genius.*

VITA'S FIRST HOME

Jane Brown

Photographs by Peter Baistow

PREVIOUS PAGE *In 1915 Vita Sackville-West and Harold Nicolson bought Long Barn, within walking distance of Knole House where Vita had grown up.*

OPPOSITE *In 1916, Vita and Harold had a barn moved from nearby to provide a fifty-foot drawing room and a writing room for Harold; it overlooks the south-facing garden.*

LEFT *The English cottage garden look was at its best during the Twenties, when Vita often entertained her Bloomsbury set friends at Long Barn.*

Vita Sackville-West and Harold Nicolson bought Long Barn, in the village of Sevenoaks Weald in Kent, in March 1915, eighteen months after they married. They had begun their life together in Constantinople, where Harold was a Secretary at the Embassy, but Vita's first pregnancy brought them back to England; and the declaration of war, two days after Ben's birth, kept them here. Long Barn was the first home of their own choosing and became a beloved refuge for fifteen years.

Vita had wanted somewhere not too far from Knole, the great house in which she grew up. Long Barn was 'a cottage on the estate' (or so Vita liked to think of it) and indeed it was within walking distance of the park and Knole House. The £2,500 they paid for Long Barn included not just the largish cottage but a few outbuildings with the remnants of a garden and a sloping field. The cottage dated from the fourteenth century: legend has it that it was William Caxton's birthplace. Before the Nicolsons acquired Long Barn, it had been rescued from dereliction by the wife of a local clergyman who, before completing the sale to Vita, built the brick terrace on the garden side of the cottage at her request.

The property grew when, early in 1916, a five-bay timber-framed barn from Brook Farm (owned by Vita's mother) was moved from across the road and added at right angles to the cottage, making an L-shaped house. In addition to dismantling and re-erecting the barn, the builders made substantial alterations to the land: they dug the field into terraces with dry-stone retaining walls to make the garden and paved some extra paths and a small parterre outside Vita's writing room window.

Although Long Barn was now a substantial house, they always referred to it as 'the cottage'. A small entrance court led into the west side of the original cottage, with hall, kitchen, dining and breakfast rooms on the left of a long paved corridor and Vita's writing room on the right with her bedroom above that. The barn provided a fifty-foot drawing room with Harold's writing room tucked away in the far corner. Upstairs were seven bedrooms and four bathrooms. The nursery establishment (the Nicolsons' second son, Nigel, was born in 1917) was based in another cottage close to the house.

Vita really moved into Long Barn in the late spring of 1916; at first it was only for

summer weekends, but gradually it commanded more and more of her time. She began her gardening, an absolute beginner, with long lists of her plans – and questions: when and how to plant lilacs? When to plant thyme, sedums, saxifrages? Which are good climbing roses? She did the usual things: sent for catalogues, looked round local nurseries, jotted down plants she liked in other people's gardens.

But, being Vita, a published poet steeped in literature, she did less usual things too, and planted the flowers celebrated in English literature – roses, daffodils, irises, wallflowers, love-in-a-mist, lavender, stocks, columbines, poppies and hollyhocks. And she went with her mother to see Gertude Jekyll at Munstead Wood in August 1917. Vita's verdict on the great gardener was 'rather fat and grumbly', but Miss Jekyll must have answered a lot of her questions and Munstead Wood itself, even in August, would have provided great inspiration.

The last war years and the early Twenties were a stormy passage in the Nicolsons' marriage, largely because of Vita's affair with Violet Trefusis, the story of which is told in Nigel Nicolson's *Portrait of a Marriage*. But by 1924 her literary reputation was growing fast and she had penetrated the Bloomsbury set as a friend of Virginia Woolf. Long Barn became an attractive venue for summer weekend parties and lingering meals on the terrace overlooking the growing garden.

Long Barn's garden was at its best, as Vita's garden, during that period – an English cottage garden with overtones of Italian sophistication. Orange and blue was her favourite colour scheme – orange tulips 'Illumination' in pots of violas or gentians, 'Orange King' roses, poppies, rudbeckias and lilies with scabious, anchusas, centaurea and lithospermums. All the terrace walls tumbled with rosemary, lavender, pinks, sedums, santolina and candytuft, with rarer treasures, tucked in corners where they prospered, of saxifrages, gentians and tiny irises brought home from her travels to the Alps and Persia.

By the spring of 1925 they had still not tackled the lowest level of the garden, below the terraces, which was very wet, even waterlogged for long periods. Harold was a particular friend and admirer of Sir Edwin Lutyens, then at the peak of his fame, spending most of his winters in India building New Delhi. It was in May that year that Lutyens came for the weekend, and with Harold devised the layout of brick-edged, raised beds for the low ground, which became known as the Dutch Garden. In the beds, built later in the summer, Vita experimented with colour schemes – a blue bed of 'Blue Jay' gladioli, meconopsis and eryngiums with white lilies, white snapdragons, all edged with white dianthus 'Mrs Sinkins'. One bed became a herb garden – as at Sissinghurst, this was nowhere near the kitchen, but then Vita was not a cook.

By 1929 the garden had come into its own. Vita still had plenty of scope for her ideas and her increasing interest in rare and tender plants – in her patch of wild, damp woodland and in the Apple Garden where she grew flowers underneath the old fruit trees. They had more or less decided that Harold would leave the diplomatic service and come home and work in England, and had it not been for a threat to use the neighbouring fields as a chicken farm they would never have considered leaving Long Barn. When Vita found Sissinghurst Castle in the spring of 1930, she fell in love with it – and its gardening possibilities – and the next Nicolson home was under way.

Since the Nicolsons sold it in 1943 Long Barn has had several owners, but it has inspired them all to treat it with care, and the garden has been tended in the spirit in which Vita made it. These pictures were taken in Dr Ione Martin's last summer there; she masterminded the garden for over ten years and handed on a healthy garden as 'living heritage'. Long Barn is a special patch of twentieth-century heritage, and for it to go on living through real lives and real families is the best possible way of conserving it.

BELOW *The clipped yews, one of Vita's earliest ideas, are a particularly striking feature of the garden.*

OPPOSITE *The layout of brick-edged raised beds for the low ground was devised by Harold and the architect Sir Edwin Lutyens during the spring of 1925.*

EDWARDIAN SPLENDOUR

Melissa Hay

Photographs by George Wright

In 1840 Henry Gibbs commissioned Gilbert Scott to build a vicarage at Clifton Hampden in Oxfordshire for his uncle, the Reverend John Gibbs. Standing on a steep rise above a bend in the river, beside the little Norman church, it must have presented a scene of exceptional tranquillity. Today, the house is owned by antiques dealer Christopher Gibbs, the great-grandson of Henry Gibbs.

Perhaps the single most dramatic incident in the history of the garden was the loss of a row of huge elms, which succumbed to Dutch elm disease during the Seventies. No longer is the garden enclosed to the south by their massive umbrageous forms and the screen from the outside world and the natural horizon that they provided is gone for ever. Since that catastrophe Christopher has reassessed the future of the garden. His plans extend well into the twenty-first century – starting with the clearance of the overgrown Victorian shrubberies. But although the house and its garden are now open to the River Thames, a bridge and an increased volume of road traffic, still they exude an air of serenity.

In the hallway of Clifton Hampden hangs a plan of the 'parsonage lands', dated 1868, showing the garden layout much as it is today – with lawns to south and west of the house, the formal garden, riverside walk, orchard and fields beyond. A photograph in a family album shows that the *Magnolia grandiflora* that covers the front of the house was already up to the eaves in the early 1900s, although a great deal of the planting dates from after the house ceased to be a vicarage in the opening years of this century.

During this period the making of the garden was carefully recorded by Lord Aldenham in a 'memoranda book' detailing important planting and the vagaries of the weather. In 1908 the river froze. In 1909 the horse chestnut was planted; in 1910 hollies and a *Wisteria multijuga* by the stables; and on 3 December 1915 the lime tree (*Tilia petiolaris*) on the lawn – now a mature and graceful tree. The winter of 1916 brought gales which blew down trees and left 'much to do in filling gaps and transplanting'.

The memoranda book draws to our attention the contribution of another member of the family – Vicary Gibbs, a plant hunter and botanist of some renown.

To the south the garden faces out across the river valley and to the west towards the church. From the lawns in front of the house the garden drops steeply to the River Thames and two statues stand guard over the prospect. Steps lead down to the riverside walk where, in spring, chionodoxas tumble in profusion down the bank, self-seeding into the paths, and snowdrops carpet the riverside. This situation presented the ideal opportunity for 'woodland' or 'wild' garden-

ABOVE *The view from the house over the lawns and the Thames valley to the Berkshire Downs and beyond.*

OPPOSITE *Two lead statues, Prince Eugène of Savoy and the Duke of Marlborough, made by Andreas Carpentier c.1720, stand guard over the south front of the house.*

PAGE 62 *The south front of the vicarage.*

PAGES 64–5 *Rose arches mark a gravel path completely overwhelmed by established herbaceous borders containing* Alchemilla mollis, *nepeta, pinks, silver thistles and* Stachys lanata.

ing, which was very much in vogue during the early years of this century.

In recent years the walk has been re-made with a stone wall retaining the massive bank of sandy soil. Now that the elms have gone and the heavy laurels have been grubbed out, its south-facing slopes are being planted with ground-cover roses, cistus and *Sorbus cashmiriana*.

On the riverside walk is the old icehouse which, having served as game larder and pumphouse in turn, is now being Gothicized to create an attractive garden building. Further along is a pair of graceful boathouses, built in 1907, and from here the path, spangled over by *Cornus mas*, makes an acute turn back up the slope towards the house. It is hoped that fritillaries will grow and self-seed in the riverside meadow and that a grove of *Salix* × 'Melanostachys' will be planted to extend the walk along and over the stream to where the river floods its banks and the native leucojums grow.

Returning by the Victorian route we come once more to the lawns where just to the east of the house, partially screened by the old yew trees, is a large plot enclosing the formal flower garden. Within this area are all the necessary and nostalgic ingredients of an English country garden at the turn of the century: velvet turf, deep borders, a rose walk, greenhouses and a cutting garden – an idyll of period charm.

In summer, roses festoon metalwork arches over a gravel path between herbaceous borders. Lacy clouds of *Crambe cordifolia* drift over the clear brilliant hues of delphiniums, phlox and roses. The whole is bounded to one side by a long pergola of rustic wood.

On the other side of the flower garden, running parallel with the pergola, is a newly planted avenue of 'red-twigged' limes (*Tilia platyphyllos* 'Corallina') underplanted with lilies of the valley and *Muscari botryoides*. At one end is an old medlar and beyond are the fruit cages and vegetable garden.

A gate leads through into an orchard where a painted statue of Bacchus stands among fruit trees, raising his glass in perpetual salute to its fecundity. Much is old and established at Clifton Hampden, much is new, a great deal is still proposed. In view of this perhaps it would be appropriate to join Bacchus in a toast to the future of this charming garden.

DIVERSE DELIGHTS

Melissa Hay

Photographs by Hugh Palmer

PAGES 68–9 *Redolent
of summer, the
herbaceous borders at
Jenkyn Place are full
of the fragrance of
roses, pinks and
lavender.*

OPPOSITE *The
perennial border in the
Leaf Garden where
hostas, euphorbias,
eryngiums and
hellebores create a
striking effect against
the backdrop of a
hornbeam hedge.*

ABOVE RIGHT *An
eighteenth-century
stone seat, the perfect
place from which to
admire the splendid
lupin borders.*

When Gerald and Patricia Coke bought Jenkyn Place, near Bentley in Hampshire, in 1941, there was just a small formal garden to the southeast of the house, some yew hedges and several interesting trees. The most notable of these was a *Liriodendron tulipifera*, now one of the largest in Britain and a magnificent spectacle when in bloom. The Cokes knew little or nothing about gardening, but they discovered that the soil conditions enabled them to indulge their quickening interest in rare and unusual plants. Now where forty years ago cows grazed, the six-acre garden contains twenty-five varieties of magnolia and a gallery of other plants.

The garden is on a belt of upper greensand, a friable sandstone giving a topsoil with distinct horticultural advantages: it is fertile and neutral, making it possible to grow both acid-loving and alkali-preferring plants.

Although not planned as a whole, the garden has evolved as such. The Cokes developed a series of separate gardens, starting with those nearest the house and then moving down over the old vegetable patch, creating vistas and axes between the various parts. A

formal Rose Garden, a highly architectural Pot Garden filled with pelargoniums, justly renowned herbaceous borders, a long rock garden and a circular Herb Garden all contrast with the loose formality of the Valley Garden and Spinney. The busy areas of colour, form and leaf shape are balanced by the simplicity and strength of the Lion Garden's long beech hedges, the Armillary Sphere Garden and the massive retaining walls of the Sunken Garden.

Jenkyn Place is stylistically a very diverse garden, but the controlling spirit is the horticultural curiosity with which it has been created. The Cokes did not set out to establish a garden of rarities but have done so inadvertently with their eye for unusual plants, which they grow in a striking manner. Space has allowed them to devote separate gardens entirely to specific conditions, ideas or times of year. The herbaceous borders are orchestrated to reach their peak at the height of summer while the Long Garden, or 'running rock garden', capitalizes on what would otherwise be a difficult situation – a dry, south-facing bank at the foot of a quickthorn hedge. Here alpines flourish in the sheltered warmth; old favourites like *Lithospermum diffusum* 'Heavenly Blue' and *Geranium sanguineum striatum* (better known as *G. lancastriense*) mingle with the esoteric evergreens of *Daphne retusa* and *Santolina neapolitana* 'Edward Bowles'. The collection of shrubs and perennials in the Leaf Garden exemplifies the Coke's fascination with foliage form and colour, the wiry leaves of *Hebe armstrongii* making a perfect foil to the shrubby willows, *Salix glaucocaerulea* and *Salix hastata* 'Wehrhahnii'.

The lower part of the garden is dedicated to autumnal colour with *Parrotia persica*, some unusual berberis and colchicums. Another surprising rarity offered by Jenkyn Place is the opportunity to see shrubs planted singly, not as 'specimen plants', but as a deliberate policy. Here, set off by fine turf with light and space all around them, each plant is able to grow to and exhibit its natural form, some – like the divinely scented *Lonicera syringantha* – reaching an unprecedented size.

A great many of the trees and shrubs at Jenkyn Place are labelled for identification and a beautifully produced illustrated guide book sensibly includes a blank page at the back for writing notes. The entire back page of mine is covered with scribbled reminders of the plants that particularly impressed me on the June day that I visited the garden – the 'Belle Portugaise' rose whose long shapely buds open to an exquisite creamy-pink flower; *Magnolia grandiflora* 'Goliath', grown as a tree rather than a wall shrub and a huge stately specimen of *Photinia serrulata* (both wonderful evergreens); the heady scent of a white wisteria (*W. venusta*); the pretty foliage and yellow flowers of *Alchemilla alpina* growing between the cracks of York paving; the exotic *Schisandra grandiflora rubrifolia*; and the glossy evergreen *Trachelospermum jasminoides*.

The contents of this astounding garden would test the most knowledgeable of plantsmen, but its charms are not only for the initiate. If you are interested in plants and want to see something you have not seen before, then this is the place for you.

BELOW *Gerald Coke at work in the herbaceous borders where scarlet poppies open their heavy heads in the sunshine.*

RIGHT *Within the shelter of old walls surrounding the Dutch Garden grow tree peonies, myrtle and roses.*

WOODLAND PARADISE

Penelope Hobhouse

Photographs by George Wright

In the steep and exposed Dorset downland between Sherborne and Dorchester, the lush gardens of Minterne Magna come as a verdant surprise.

The grounds of Minterne Magna fall abruptly into two deep valleys, both of which stretch south and curve gently round to an open view of parkland beyond. The soil here is fertile greensand, watered by natural springs. A total contrast to the chalky downs scarcely a few hundred yards away.

The luxuriant planting at Minterne reflects five generations of the Digby family's horticultural knowledge and application. Individual tree and shrub specimens also trace the chronological history of plant introductions to England, in particular, hybridization of rhododendrons.

The property passed from the Churchills to Admiral Robert Digby in 1768. The Admiral, a Digby from Sherborne Castle, found the landscape bleak, as he wrote in his journal of

that year: 'I visited my new estate, valley very bare, trees not thriving, house ill contrived and ill situated.'

His first task was to plant shelter belts on the main ridges where today his groves, mainly of beech and some fine old Scots pines and cedars of Lebanon, dominate the setting of the house. In addition to filtering wind, they provide the essential canopy and leaf-mould mulch for the gardens in the lower valley. Admiral Digby also transformed the property in another way, which proved to be crucial to the beauty and interest of the estate.

Finding natural water at the head of the valley to the north-east of the house, he built a series of fourteen dams and rocky cascades at descending levels, creating a broad stretch of water immediately below the house. Over this he constructed an elegant balustraded bridge. These works were completed in the 1780s and the lower course of the stream adds

ABOVE *The house stands to the north of the valley gardens.*

PREVIOUS PAGE *Minterne Magna's sheltered landscape provides a haven for luxuriant planting, helped by an average annual rainfall of forty-two inches.*

The beauty of Minterne's famed rhododendron woods is greatly enhanced by water in still pools above the steep cascades.

RIGHT *Above the eighteenth-century bridge the valley opens out and planting becomes more naturalistic.*

much to the charm and beauty of the rhododendron wood, where the constant sound of water cools and refreshes. The banks are planted with the textured foliage of moisture-loving plants.

So Minterne has two interlocking landscapes. The classical eighteenth-century view looking east over the bridge certainly reflects the influence of 'Capability' Brown who, during the 1750s, worked at Sherborne Castle for the Admiral's father. The two lower valley gardens, one of which follows the stream bed and the other separated from it by a high ridge further to the west, both curve round to the south to make a horseshoe shape. Steep-sided banks and the valley bottoms provide a sheltered spot for luxuriant planting, helped by an average annual rainfall of forty-two inches.

By the end of the nineteenth century, woodland gardening became almost synonymous with the planting of rhododendrons. Sir Joseph Hooker's introductions from Nepal were welcome additions to *R. arboreum* in the early years of that century. At Minterne, hardy bamboos were planted in drifts in the hanging woodland as extra shelter for the tender large-leaved rhododendrons. Today, the bamboos have spread, their pale rustling foliage contrasting so well with that of the heavier rhododendrons.

The rhododendron collection grew – seed came from the great plant collectors of the first half of this century. The *nobleanum* hybrids, which flower in early spring, are well represented at Minterne. 'Christmas Cheer' has white flower trusses opening from pink buds. A hybrid such as *R.* × *cinnkeyes* (a cross between *cinnabarinum* and *keysii*) flowers in late May with red, yellow-flushed flowers. A large specimen of *R.* 'Polar Bear' has white flowers in July scenting the whole garden. Sadly, the 1976 drought destroyed many of the larger-leaved rhododendrons, but replacement seedlings are now growing away.

Although best known for its rhododendrons, Minterne supports many other trees and shrubs. An avenue of Japanese cherries lines the western path; tall specimens of the pocket-handkerchief tree *Davidia involucrata* jostle with enkianthus, pieris, maples and magnolias. Across a wiggle in the stream the coral-pink branches of *Acer palmatum* 'Senkaki' are vivid in winter, outlined against a backdrop of more solid greens.

There are several trees of the early-flowering *Magnolia campbellii mollicomata* which wait twenty years to mature and

flower, and *M.* × *soulangiana* which flowers reliably each April. Round a corner clumps of Chusan palm, *Trachycarpus fortunei*, come as an exotic surprise in the Dorset landscape. Aconites, snowdrops and narcissi carpet the ground in spring; later astilbes, hemerocallis and rodgersias provide clusters of colour by the stream. Bridges and stepping stones connect the sloping banks where gunnera and skunk cabbage thrive.

Visitors are welcome from April to October. The best route to follow is anti-clockwise, starting at the southern front of the great Edwardian house, before a wide view framed by an old cedar of Lebanon and a tall deodar (*Cedrus deodara*) planted to commemorate the birth of the present Lord Digby in 1924. A specimen *Abies koreana* with purple cones dates from the birth of his son; a golden-leaved deodar, celebrating a grandson, awaits a site. Stretching southwards are lime trees and beech woods. Suddenly the path drops down into the first valley, curving away to the far end of the woodland garden where it joins the lowest cascade. The homeward track takes you north again mainly along the stream, with the bridge coming into view above the highest dam at the head of the valley.

What makes Minterne unique is the continuity of interest shown in it by successive generations of Digbys. It must be rare for a gardening family to act with such aesthetic and botanical unanimity of spirit. The result is a most carefully contrived and fascinating garden – and one that is continuing to flourish.

This is a garden for all seasons. In spring, specimens of sycamore (*Acer pseudoplatanus* 'Brilliantissimum') with leaves of vivid shrimp pink stand out against more sober greens. The foliage of the swamp cypress, *Taxodium distichum*, turns from fresh green to brownish pink in October, when a *Parrotia persica* with its mottled bark has leaves of a rich crimson. Beside it the sugary fragrant leaves of a *Cercidiphyllum japonicum* turn to pink and yellow.

'Wild' gardening is the most difficult of stylistic forms – the essence of woodland planting is the apparent freedom. At Minterne, the Brownian landscape and the Edwardian woodland flow together as one coherent scheme. One is almost austere in its classical simplicity, the other has the intimacy and charm of a family garden reflecting so much the taste and inspiration of those who have tended it.

Bluebells carpet the ground beside the upper banks of the stream.

The view from Admiral Robert Digby's classical bridge reveals some of the rare trees and shrubs growing in the sheltered valley below.

THE HEALING ART
Penelope Hobhouse
Photographs by Hugh Palmer

During the Second World War, Peter Healing was a prisoner in Germany. He had access to just one book, *The English Flower Garden*, written by William Robinson in 1883. The chapter 'Colour in the Flower Garden' especially took his interest:

> Splendid harmonies of rich and brilliant colour, and proper sequences of such harmonies, should be the rule; there should be large effects, each well studied and well placed . . . It is important . . . that the mass of each colour should be large enough to have a certain dignity, but not so large as to be wearisome . . . In sunny places warm colours should preponderate; the yellow colour of sunlight brings them together and adds to their glowing effect . . . A shady border . . . seems best suited for the cooler more delicate colours.

Today, the established luxuriance of Mr and Mrs Healing's skilfully planned borders reflects Robinson's message to perfection.

The four-acre garden frames an elegant eighteenth-century house on the south-facing slopes of Bredon Hill, looking across the Bristol Channel and the Welsh hills. The sticky clay soil has a pH of seven to eight; over the years texture has been improved by humus-forming mulch, and digging is never necessary. In the 1940s there were few trees; today walnuts, maples and mulberries give the garden scale and character. Borders are

planned in a series of colour harmonies for a long summer display from June to the first frosts. But it is not only the colour planning that makes the gardens at The Priory so completely satisfying. Each individual plant is chosen for some indefinable quality of excellence, which depends on Mr and Mrs Healing's finely balanced judgement. In addition, each plant is well grown and thrives in its situation.

The main border, a smaller parallel border close to the house and a third, lying below the ruins of the old priory, were planned during Peter's captivity. Basic flower and foliage harmonies are augmented by annuals and tender plants – the colours remain the same, though the plants may be different each year. Peter likes to experiment with form, too: contrasts between leaf shape and plant form contribute to balanced compositions. Sword-like leaves of phormiums, crocosmias and kniphofias act as foils to the more relaxed curves of shrubs and clumps of perennials. Each border or section is a complete pictorial composition.

At either end of the main border, which is 180 feet long and eighteen feet wide, pale silvery- and grey-foliaged plants make a tapestry frame for flowers in pastel tints or tinted whites. Towards the centre, the stronger yellow of *Achillea* 'Coronation Gold' builds up to the rusty oranges, browns and reds of daisy-flowered helianthus, and the

deeper scarlet of *Lobelia* 'Dark Crusader' grouped in front of the claret-leaved *Cotinus coggygria* 'Foliis Purpureis'. Beyond, colours cool to misty mauves, yellows and creams, set off by silvery thistles and thalictrums.

In the border by the house, groups of white roses are separated by drifts of flowers in pink, mauve, purple and blue. Rampant white Japanese anemones spread at the back. Pink and white dahlias and scented tobacco plants (including the stately white-flowered *Nicotiana sylvestris*) are annual additions. Lavender-blue *Aster × frikartii* and *A. sedifolius* grow next to grey- and silver-leaved artemisias, helichrysums and perovskias.

Hidden at first from view, the third border is a total contrast. There are plants in every shade of red and bronze, dark reds and purplish leaves absorbing the heat of the more garish scarlets. Bronze-leaved scarlet *Dahlia* 'Bishop of Llandaff' jostles crimson *Nicotiana* 'Dark Red' and *Penstemon* 'Firebird'; low-growing *Iresine herbstii* is a neighbour to the startling red-stemmed ruby chard. Old red roses, penstemons, monardas backed by purple-leaved nut and dark-leaved smoke bushes and berberis make the border, in Peter's words, 'overflow like a cornucopia'.

Behind a dark yew hedge is a secret garden area, geared for peak performance in June. Small trees like *Acer griseum* with peeling bark, a Judas tree, golden-leaved *Gleditsia triacanthos* 'Sunburst' give height. Philadelphus bushes with heavy-scented white and creamy flowers spread above hardy perennials, bulbs and tall grasses. Here, gentle grey-leaved plants with pale flower colouring spill over a central path, at one end of which a sundial makes a focal point. To the north this hidden garden is closed in by a broad pergola, its upright pillars and roof clothed alternately in clinging vines and climbing roses. In summer, this shady walk, running across the garden, offers a welcoming cool contrast to the dazzling sunlit lawns and colourful beds.

The Healings also love to grow unusual plants, and among those on sale to visitors are rare kniphofias and salvias, blue penstemons and silver-leaved shrubby *Lupinus albifrons*, not easily obtained elsewhere.

At The Priory each plant plays its role in a carefully orchestrated architectural and colour composition. To achieve such perfection requires not only considerable aesthetic judgement, but also horticultural skills of a high order. New generations of gardeners will draw inspiration from a garden of such quality.

PREVIOUS PAGE *The overflowing midsummer borders.*

ABOVE *Rare plants thrive around the sunken garden.*

BELOW *Misty catmint growing in front of yellow-flowered phlomis.*

OPPOSITE *Salvias with dahlias and nicotiana.*

RISING PROSPECTS

Ethne Clarke

Photographs by Hugh Palmer

British gardens are the envy of the world. The greatest are now maintained by such bodies as the National Trust; others owe their survival to the efforts of their devoted owners, who often tend them as part of a family legacy. One such garden is at Chidmere House, West Sussex, planted in 1930 by the late H. L. Baxendale, father of the present owner, Tom Baxendale. In five and a half acres surrounding the Tudor house, he laid out a garden modelled on Hidcote Gardens in Gloucestershire. 'Rooms' formed by high hornbeam hedges and clipped yews, eye-catching vistas across the gardens and a succession of changing views all set the Hidcote stamp on Chidmere.

When the Baxendales arrived the house was tumbledown and the grounds consisted of a scruffy cabbage patch, a derelict orchard and a few ploughed fields; there were no trees, and salty winds blew in from the Channel five miles away. The mere or lake, from which the house takes its name, was somewhat choked and marshy.

Over five years the gardens took shape. Woodland cherry, Norway maple and silver birch trees were planted to make a boundary screen, and the hornbeam hedges were set out to lend shelter and provide a framework for further planting. The mere was improved, and its garden bank studded with bog- and water-loving plants. Today, the lake gives sanctuary to a wide variety of wildfowl.

Appropriately, the formal elements of the garden were sited nearest the house, melting away into informal woodland and shrubbery. The central axes of the garden cross at right angles, with paths meandering off through the orchard and shrubbery and into the numerous individual gardens. Decorative urns and statues, purchased at the Paris Exhibition of 1867 by Tom's great-grandfather, define the way.

The gardens are much the same today, the only dramatic change being the alteration of one area of formal beds. The tree screen behind had reached full maturity and overshadowed the plants below, so the beds were taken out, leaving a large area of the garden easier to tend. Only the larger shrubs such as lilacs and tree peonies were retained, and a number of old-fashioned shrub roses were planted. This list is quite impressive and includes 'Penelope', 'Honorine de Brabant', 'Roseraie de l'Hay', *Rosa mundi* and 'Blanc Double de Coubert'. Otherwise Tom maintains the garden as his father conceived it.

Even so, I was delighted to come upon a recent innovation: a small formal bed within one of the areas enclosed by hornbeam hedges. Edged with box and planted with bay and other herbs, it hints at a knot garden, which is fitting given the period of the house. An especially pleasing element of the new bed are two young cypress trees raised from seed that Tom carried home with him from Italy

and nurtured in the heavy Sussex clay and the shelter of a warm corner.

The same soil is unsuitable for rhododendrons, azaleas and camellias. in spite of this, Tom's predecessor did manage to plant a special bed of the first two. Tom regrets that there are no camellias but, even so, there is plenty to please him. For instance – tulips. Nearly twenty years ago, the gardener put in a mass of parrot tulip bulbs against the front of the house: planted nine to twelve inches deep, rather than the usual four, they have flourished and increased in the heavy soil.

PREVIOUS PAGE *View from the centre of the garden to the gatehouse.*

ABOVE *A clump of* Phormium tenax *provides a dramatic vertical line..*

Tom's inclination towards formality and his love of Italian gardens have produced a potting shed that is one of a kind. The classical columns either side of the entrance make an amusingly grand façade for what is usually an undistinguished building.

Chidmere is a brilliant spring-time garden. There are banks of *Anemone blanda*, with lush carpets of grape hyacinths and daffodils (now naturalized) in the woodland and orchard beneath apple, pear and plum trees. March through May sees the peak of floral beauty, thanks to unusual specimen trees such as *Halesia carolina* (the North American snowdrop tree), *Davidia involucrata* (the pocket-

handkerchief tree) and *Cornus kousa chinensis*, as well as flowering cherries, numerous magnolias and the early-flowering old-fashioned roses. But Tom is gradually introducing plants that will reduce the spring emphasis and provide more interest in summer and early autumn. The winds and rains of an English spring, he feels, make a garden difficult to enjoy.

One of the present summer highlights, and something that gives Tom great pleasure, is the greenhouse at the lake's edge, well stocked with exotics. Orchids and mimosa, strelitzia and datura grow beneath geraniums

LEFT *Cerise aubrieta grows at the base of clipped yew pillars at the gatehouse end of the first avenue.*

ABOVE Rubus cockburnianus, *in spring it has fern-like leaves, in June small purple flowers followed by black bloomy fruits.*

that cover the back wall, and a small lemon tree provides all the fruit needed by the house.

Passing through the greenhouse, you come to the boating platform, where on summer evenings Tom likes to linger beneath a deep-purple-leaved grapevine, enjoying the tranquillity of the lake. He regards gardening as 'good therapy', welcome relaxation after a week working in London.

Chidmere recently celebrated its golden anniversary with the National Gardens Scheme; every summer for over fifty years, the Baxendale family has opened the gardens to the public in aid of this charity.

CREATIVE CONVERSIONS

Who has not wanted to buy a ruined barn and turn it, by dint of skill and imagination, into a perfect, tailor-made home? Even more than renovating and redecorating an existing house, such a labour takes time, patience, and usually a great deal of money – but the final rewards are greater still.

Some clever spirits are able to build something out of nothing. Artist Graham Ovenden is a case in point, creating from a ramshackle Cornish cottage a quite remarkable Gothic fantasy – and all with his own hands and minimal labour costs.

There are conversions that look unprepossessing from the outside and yet inside contain an Aladdin's cave of riches – such a house is the Quaker meeting house in Devizes which anyone might pass without a second glance. Chapels are popular conversions, for they have a comfortingly religious look and reassuring atmosphere that often linger after deconsecration.

Perhaps most exotic of all is the castle in Ireland which seems almost hewn out of the raw rock and yet, for all that, has evolved into a welcoming, if unusual, family home.

All the beauty we associate with English houses is here, but added to it is the marvellous individuality which we also recognize as our own.

OPPOSITE *Heale Hall; the drawing room*
leads to a conservatory created
from an old lean-to.

THE MAKING OF HEALE HALL

Kate Corbett-Winder

Photographs by Timothy Beddow

Lesley and Jonathan Heale live and work at Heale Hall. Not their ancestral seat, but a converted Victorian schoolroom in Montgomery, a peaceful town on the Welsh borders. It was built by the Presbyterian Chapel in 1882 for their Sunday school and when attendances fell, was used for functions by local societies. When the Chapel put it up for auction in 1979, the Heales realized it had the makings of a studio. Both artists, they had left London for Wales in the mid-Seventies to share Julie Christie's farmhouse and use her barns as studios.

Bidding for the schoolroom – on the premises – started at £4,000 and went up in hundreds to £8,250. It sounds a low price, even for seven years ago, but it was just a shell. 'We stopped counting the cost when it reached £20,000,' says Lesley. The Heales had bought what was effectively a forty-foot granite box with soaring vaulted ceiling and institutional leaded windows. Having intended to use the schoolroom as a studio, Lesley and Jonathan decided to make it home as well for them and their children.

The Heales were in no hurry to move in. Jonathan made a doll's-house-size cardboard model and they experimented with the layout for a year before starting building. When things began, Jonathan did the supervising and much of the work himself. At first it was a relatively slow process but it snowballed gradually; then more help was recruited to make Heale Hall habitable.

The place was a brave undertaking, with fundamental alterations crying out to be done before any interior work could start. In spite of the auctioneer's assurance, recent roof repairs, for example, were only make-shift patches and the damp areas on the ceiling grew ominously until the only answer was to renew all the lead.

Inside, an upstairs floor and staircase were the major requirements. Then they constructed a platform at one end of the interior, supported by a wooden column and beams fixed into the roof trusses; these hold up an overhanging balcony bedroom with a deep corner window – straight out of *Romeo and Juliet*. The original plan was to have two bedrooms side by side, but Lesley and Jonathan could not resist using the whole space and built another staircase to make an attic bedroom for their children.

Downstairs, priority of space has gone to the 'living studio' (known as 'outside' in winter because of the temperature). This is an area measuring almost twenty-five foot square with a wooden floor. It has work elements in one half – a massive workbench, materials, kiln, china, books and assorted artistic clutter – and drawing room in the other. There is an invisible division, but an inevitable overlap most of the time.

The kitchen is underneath the balcony

bedroom. It is light, thanks to the glass in the panelling, but has a low ceiling. The library at the other end has a future bedroom above it, but no stairs have yet been built.

The studio has an air of creativity. Jonathan illustrates children's books, paints or prints woodcuts on a Victorian printing press. Lesley is responsible for the striking profusion of curtains, cushions, upholstery and screens painted in her bold style.

Yoking their originality to the formality of a Victorian Arts and Crafts building has worked triumphantly. 'We've been slaves to the architectural style of the place,' says Jonathan, 'making a feature of the roof trusses, painting the flowers which decorate the ceiling, making cupboards from leaded windows.' It is a clever mix of styles: the austere institutional space with a lavish, almost theatrical finish. Allergic to newness, they have gone to great lengths to achieve a worn, comfortable feel without letting things look self-consciously antique. 'We love the way paint changes colour with age and wear,' explains Jonathan.

The panelled walls in the studio are painted

PAGE 90 *High ceilings and enormous windows provide good natural light for the studio space.*

a milky mint green. The vast expanse from roof to panelling is a pale grey with a faint yellow stripe – achieved by dribbling lines of paint from a great height, fed by a battery-driven syringe. The yellow colouring, diluted with emulsion, is sheep raddle – the bright marking paint daubed on to a ram's harness in the tupping season!

Despite a rural existence surrounded by rolling hills, pigs and sheep, Lesley and Jonathan keep strong city links and friends now gather at Heale Hall as if it were an out-of-town Chelsea Arts Club.

They are both very versatile and successful artists, never restricting themselves to one medium or surface. They often work together, sharing commissions and putting on joint exhibitions. Because they trained in different techniques (Lesley in paint and textiles, Jonathan in typography, print and paint – at Chelsea Art School, then the Royal College), their combined talents are a strong force on china, cloth, canvas or paper. They most enjoy working to fairly open commissions. 'It is ideal to be given *carte blanche* on the strength of work you've already done. The bliss is being able to stay here to do the job and work whatever hours you choose.'

But life is not all work. It goes in cycles of all-out activity on what is half-seriously called the 'HCP', 'the "high creative plane"'. Getting there can take time, but it's great when you've eventually reached it.' Then, inevitably, there follows a wholehearted slump.

Lesley and Jonathan are spontaneous travellers, ready to rush to a wedding in California or a party in London. But moving from the country is out of the question. 'We can't imagine a house as perfect as this in London,' says Jonathan. 'We do depend on city money for commissions, but it's heaven to come back here. We can always visit any city. After all, you might as well drive to Heathrow from here as from Hammersmith.'

It is certainly a much prettier drive.

LEFT *A collection of prints and plates line the walls of the library, another hive of creative activity at Heale Hall.*

BELOW *French windows open from the kitchen on to a quarry-tiled area protected by a glass roof.*

PREACHING
TO THE CONVERTED

Rosalind Burdett

Photographs by Timothy Beddow

The charming Wiltshire home of interior decorator Jo Robinson is far from the austere Wesleyan chapel it was until twenty years ago. Comfortable squashy sofas replace hard wooden pews; the original vestry is now a well-planned kitchen-dining room; and the outhouse which used to house the preacher's pony and trap now forms a charming guest room.

The tranquillity usually found in a chapel remains, however, and Jo delights in having such a peaceful weekend retreat from city life. Although her teenage daughters also appreciate the calm, they often visit the chapel on their own to spend weekends with their friends – they say the house is ideal for parties.

Some years ago, Jo and her daughters were looking for a weekend home in Wiltshire. The family has had ties with the district for a long time; Jo's great-great-grandfather lived in the next village and he might even have passed the chapel when it was being built in 1895.

'Chapels conjure up visions of damp, cold places with graves in the garden,' says Jo. But when she went to see it, she discovered that part of the building had already been converted and had been used as a home, although the chapel itself was little altered and some of the original pews were still in place. The vestry had been used as an all-in-one living room, and the outhouse and stable had been joined to the house to make an extra bedroom.

While its owners had carried out no work on the chapel, they had done a great deal to the garden. They had planted many old-fashioned roses, honeysuckles and apple trees, making a charming cottage garden. Today the garden is still well tended: a local man, Albert Tancock, does most of the work while Jo takes pride in caring for the magnificent box hedges.

To realize the potential in the original building took enormous vision. But Jo, an interior designer, has plenty of that. With the help of her architect cousin, Robert Townsend, she set to work to convert the chapel into a home tailor-made for her requirements.

Jo was keen to take advantage of the whole of the attractive building and its original features. The chapel has a superb oak parquet floor and a pine dado all around the walls, including the vestry. The lovely arched windows have soft-coloured stained glass, all intact; around the doors are Oxford architraves; and the vaulted ceiling has impressive crossbeams. Robert and Jo worked out the best way of installing bedrooms and bathrooms without losing the character of the building. Robert drew up the plans and employed a local firm of builders which has an excellent team of carpenters. 'All the work went very smoothly,' Jo says with visible relief – mainly thanks to good planning, she

feels. 'I had worked out beforehand precisely what I wanted and I made sure the builders did exactly as I requested.' The only real problem was having to travel from her London home in order to keep an eye on the work. But as the conversion was done in six months, that particular inconvenience did not last unbearably long.

In order to create an entrance hall as well as an extra room, a gallery was built over what had originally been the entrance. The front door was moved from its central position and is now at the corner of the new hall. The original porch has been converted into a

PREVIOUS PAGE *In the sitting room, the exposed roof timbers help to retain the ecclesiastical character of the building.*

cloakroom and the gallery (a platform where the girls sleep), which forms the ceiling in the hall, is reached by a custom-built cast-iron spiral staircase.

In the hallway, the carpenters built pine shelves to hold books and hi-fi equipment. Stained to match the original dado, the shelves blend in well – giving interest to the hallway and a home for what might clutter up the sitting room. An archway was also built, echoing the shape of the windows; this has been stained black.

The main area of the chapel forms the sitting room and the roof has been left as it was, with the vaulted beams exposed to preserve the ecclesiastical feel. The large

BELOW *A fine nineteenth-century secretaire takes pride of place between two large casement windows in the main bedroom; backs of pews salvaged from the chapel embellish the half-wall of the gallery.*

ABOVE *From the informal dining room, once the vestry, french windows open out to the garden.*

windows are uncurtained as Jo felt that curtains would detract from their simplicity. The wood-burning stove, which heats the house, is both cosy and practical and is surrounded by deep sofas and colourful antique rugs.

The vestry – now the kitchen-dining room – was an attractively proportioned room with a pretty cast-iron fireplace set in a corner and a lovely wooden floor. These features were both retained, but french windows now open on to the garden. The pine kitchen units, again stained to match the dado, harmonize so perfectly that they might always have been there and the large refectory table – with an unusual set of bentwood chairs – makes this a pleasant and informal dining room.

From the sitting room, the main bedroom is approached by a pretty Edwardian staircase installed by Jo. It was also stained to tone with the original pine dado. As for the upper landing, the bedroom doorway was designed to match the rest of the woodwork and the door is an undetectable replica of others. It makes a perfect gallery for a collection of family portraits, ranging from one of Jo's grandmother, drawn in charcoal by her governess at the turn of the century, to an oil painting of her great-grandmother and her cousin.

Jo realized that the chapel was not big enough to accommodate friends as well as family, so an extension to the main bedroom and bathroom-dressing room was skilfully and sympathetically built out over the vestry. Externally, it is covered in old terracotta tile cladding, mixing happily with the rest of the building's warm, red brick. The two large casement windows – between which an exquisite nineteenth-century secretaire has pride of place – give a wonderful view of the surrounding countryside running down to the river, and the floral curtains work well with the antique English patchwork quilt and the lace tablecloth covering the bedside table. To house extra clothes and guests' belongings, there are two runs of spacious wardrobes – one in the bedroom, one in the dressing room.

After all the time and care lavished on it, the chapel is now worth something approaching double its value when Jo bought it – although any price that might be placed on it is theoretical, as Jo is adamant that it will remain in the family for years to come. They obviously love the tranquillity of their chapel home and extol its virtues to all their visitors, who never need convincing. You could say they are preaching to the converted.

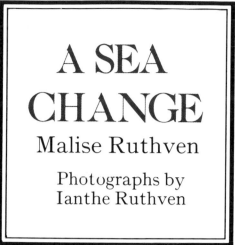

A SEA CHANGE
Malise Ruthven

Photographs by Ianthe Ruthven

T he castle faces due west over the Atlantic, a tall stark sentinel guarding the shores of Europe against the constant winds and storms. At high tide the waters surround its lower battlements on three sides. During hurricane-force gales, the waves crash around the walls of the keep itself and it would be suicidal to venture up on the roof.

Like the other square towers on this part of the west coast of Ireland, it was built by Norman settlers in the thirteenth century to command the road and act as a stronghold from which the Norman knights and their henchmen could subdue the local Gaelic tribes. But it gradually passed into native Irish ownership: cut off from their base in England by hundreds of miles of forest, swamp and sea, the Normans soon became 'more Irish than the Irish themselves'. The castle last saw military action in the 1650s during Oliver Cromwell's brutal and bloody Irish campaign. Fortunately for Alec and Leonie Finn the walls were not wrecked by the English artillery.

When Leonie's mother, writer Anita Leslie, bought the castle shortly after the Second World War it had long been a derelict ruin. The keep, with a nearby field, cost her less than £200. She paid for the construction of a new flat roof and other essentials by selling an emerald ring – the gift of her American mother, a cousin of Winston Churchill. She

PREVIOUS PAGE *The castle, on the west coast of Ireland, is spectacularly sited facing out over the Atlantic.*

LEFT *The main upper room of the keep, once a soldiers' dormitory, is now a guest bedroom.*

ABOVE *The comfortable living room in the two-storey cottage built next to the keep.*

and her yachtsman husband, Commander Bill King, did the keep up, bit by bit over the years, between bouts of hunting and ocean racing.

The tower was never exactly comfortable. The Kings failed to conquer the damp – a major cause being the flat roof. 'We would like to have put on a gabled roof with slates,' explains Bill, 'but there just wasn't enough money. The tower has always been soaking, though it's been slightly better recently. When we first came, it actually used to rain

indoors. You could stand inside the great hall and see a fine mist gently falling down.'

The damp has encouraged a profusion of plants to flourish indoors without any assistance from pots or watering cans. Ferns and wild flowers grow quite naturally out of the walls – or you can see them in the crevices under the arrow slits. In one of the small vaulted rooms, the whole of the area round the window has become an exotic palm house, with several species of fern nurtured by what looks like centuries of greenish water seeping

down the walls. 'It's very easy to clean the castle,' says Alec. 'You don't have to bother with things like the wallpaper peeling off.'

Constant damp and the dangers of dark unlit stairways with steep, narrow steps persuaded the Kings to move out while the children were small, and to build themselves a cottage nearby. Bill had the cottage built according to his and Anita's drawings, while he was sailing in the Caribbean. When he came back he found that the house had been built following his plans, but facing the wrong direction. However, they happened on a piece of good luck (or for Catholic Anita, perhaps, divine intervention). One day she saw some workmen beginning to demolish the local Protestant church, which had been deserted by its parishioners. The fine cut granite stones, which exactly matched those of the castle, were being crushed for road filler. Anita bargained with the foreman and a deal was struck: she bought all the remaining stones for two and sixpence each. Using a local mason, but without an architect, she built a comfortable two-storey block adjoining the keep. The new building, with its low profile and small windows, blends well with the rest of the castle.

Alec and Leonie moved into the comfortable part of the castle, along with their two children, after Anita's death. Alec is lead guitarist and bouzouki player with Dé Danann, one of Ireland's leading folk-groups; Leonie, a painter, teaches at a nearby art college. Although Alec's family originally came from Galway, he grew up in Yorkshire and seems to have stiffened his Irish imagination with a touch of North Country grit. His passion for falconry (as well as the drink, he adds, with a laugh) brought him back to the land of his ancestors. 'It's very difficult to go hawking in Britain,' he says. 'All the moors are let out for shooting, so English falconers have to pay a lot of money to rent their own patch, in places like Caithness. Then there are all those gamekeepers and "no trespassing" signs. Here I can take my birds out on the bog and go where I please.' He is also a parrot fancier and is building a large aviary in the garden which will be cunningly concealed under the castle walls.

Alec has ambitious plans for the keep. 'I'm going to put hidden storage heaters in every room,' he says, 'to dry the place out properly. Then we'll go through the rooms, one by one, to make sure each has the right kind of furniture. We'll put proper electric lights in the great hall. We'll try to do it cleverly by getting some of those nice old Moroccan lamps. Then it will actually be possible to go in there and sit and be warm and comfortable.'

'You'll have to find a million pounds, plus VAT,' says Bill. But Alec is not deterred by his father-in-law's scepticism. He hopes to get repair grants from the Government and open the castle to the public for one month in the year to qualify for tax relief. He will find plenty of local people to point the outside walls, which have never been properly done.

'You'll still have to dry out the inside,' says Bill. The walls are so thick that this could easily take decades to achieve.

There is one thing, however, on which everyone is agreed. The keep, with its fine old medieval hall, is ideal for parties. You can make a huge blaze in the fireplace – and the chimney is so well constructed that it never smokes, even in a gale. And the acoustics – according to Alec – are wonderful. It is the finest place for miles around for weddings, dances and – who knows? – even wakes.

As we are leaving, a party is in preparation for a neighbour's daughter. The old trestle table groans with hams, salmon, canapés. The archways are stocked with crates of beer, wine and stout. The candles are lit. As the westering sun sends shafts of gold dancing off the sea and on to the craggy walls, the guests begin to arrive.

OPPOSITE *The great hall is furnished in a style evoking the castle's Norman and Gaelic builders.*

BELOW *A window decorated with plants in the passageway connecting the Norman keep with the modern living quarters.*

A TRIUMPHAL APPROACH

Julie Woodgate

Photographs by Christopher Drake

'Follow the narrow lane through the trees until you come to the spot where five roads converge, cross them bearing right and there it is – you can't miss it.'

Indeed you cannot, for there, spanning an impossibly straight and endless drive, is its stark, geometric outline standing out in sharp relief against the rounded contours of the surrounding north Norfolk landscape. The arch was designed in the 1730s by William Kent – and constructed over the next thirty years in conjunction with the building of the big house, Holkham Hall. It was intended as a fitting prelude to the glories of Holkham from the southern approach, a delightful frontispiece to the estate as a whole and a handy hunting lodge. Later, the northern entrance was more favoured by visitors, so the arch became neglected, falling into disrepair. And that is how architect Nicholas Hills found it during a holiday in nearby Wells-next-the-Sea some fifteen years ago. Immediately enchanted by the thought of living in such a place, he wrote to Viscount Coke, DL, for permission to rent it. Two years later, after he had been thoroughly vetted and finally approved, he moved in.

The triumphal arch stands just outside the walled part of the Hall. Nicholas comments: 'It's rather like having the whole of Hyde Park to yourself – you don't have to see anyone if you don't want to.' Lord Coke maintains and farms the huge estate as his ancestors did, and consequently many of the buildings retain their original function. At Longlands, the building works department, G.A.Dean's 'model' buildings from the 1860s still house a blacksmith's shop, a carpenter's shop and all the necessary workshops for the large home farm. Nearby is Nicholas's office, from which he runs his busy architectural practice, renovating and redesigning houses, hotels and other buildings around the country – including the James Wyatt-designed Palmer's Lodge, another gatehouse on the Holkham estate. In this respect, he is an ideal tenant for the arch. The arrangement he has with Holkham is mutually advantageous, for in addition to the peppercorn rent he is responsible for all repairs and restoration and keeping the arch insured.

When he moved in, it had been empty for over fifty years. There was no water or electricity, the windows were boarded up and in the right leg of the arch, the stairs and intermediate floor had gone. At some stage, the building had been reroofed and all the chimneys sealed, so Nicholas had to rebuild these. He also rebuilt the stairs and floor in the right leg, thus creating two small guest bedrooms which, together with the lavatory and shower he installed, constitute what, following the tradition of the Hall, he calls the 'Strangers' Wing'. He had water piped through from the cattle trough on the other

PAGE 104 *At the southern approach to Holkham Hall in Norfolk stands the triumphal-arch home of architect Nicholas Hills.*

The main room that spans the arch with (ABOVE) *the south-facing semi-circular window giving a spectacular view along the drive and* (RIGHT) *the bookshelves commissioned to echo the design of the obelisk also by William Kent on the Holkham estate.*

LEFT *Nicholas Hills hand-tinting a copy of Kent's original design for the arch.*

LEFT *The yellow kitchen, with reminders of the building's past use as a hunting lodge.*

ABOVE *Guarding the door of the Strangers' Wing.*

side of the field but, as yet, has no electricity. 'I hadn't realized before just how much work having no electricity creates: collecting wood, splitting logs for fuel, making and trimming candles, filling oil lamps and a tremendous amount of dusting. I sometimes feel I'm living in the eighteenth century.'

The left leg houses the kitchen where Nicholas tiled over the original concrete floor and built a gallery as a dressing room-cum-storage area and installed a shower and lavatory. It is up the stone spiral staircase on this side that you gain access to the large room that spans the arch. Here, he has made a sofabed from four covered quarters of foam which open out to form a circular bed or fold to make a semi-circular seat that reflects the shape of the lunette window directly behind it. The bookshelves standing sentinel either side of the sofabed were commissioned to echo the design of the William Kent obelisk further up the drive, and conceal a battery-operated car radio and television.

Nicholas's ingenious use of space has created a home that seems the ideal site for one man, his dog and the occasional visitor, so it is hard to believe that the arch was once occupied by two families – one in each leg, with the central room partitioned into three communal bedrooms.

The setting is idyllic, the service delightfully rustic. The postman drops the mail through the lavatory window on his way up to the Hall; the dustman pops in when he is passing. Along the drive beyond the arch – where the avenue of oak trees was reputedly grown from the acorns used as packing material for shipments of sculpture from Italy – the penned sheep are slowly moved along the grassy verges to keep the grazing even. As you approach the arch, baleful cattle scatter before you to regroup and moo belligerently from a safe distance, until their inquisitiveness overcomes their fear and they amble over to investigate any belongings misguidedly left outside. Nicholas's broken garden furniture and trampled flowerpots testify to their past curiosity.

He says: 'I do have permission to fence this off and keep the wretched cattle out, but on the other hand there is something delicious about living in a field, don't you think?'

GOTHIC FANTASY

Suzanne Askham

Photographs by Simon Brown

L ondon does not even figure in the vocabulary. The wooden platform indicator for eastbound trains at Bodmin Parkway Station simply says *Liskeard, Plymouth and Beyond*. The rest of England, east of Devon's western tip, is thus neatly dismissed in a single mysterious word, and the capital itself lies forgotten, and unregretted, somewhere beneath the horizon.

It was this distance that first drew artist Graham Ovenden to Cornwall some thirteen years ago. 'I wanted to get as far away from London as possible.' As Graham is one of England's leading Ruralist painters and as ruralism is all about getting back to the countryside, the move was not entirely unexpected. But even so, Ovenden's change of address has been more extraordinary than most – from a modest, nondescript semidetached house in the London suburb of Hounslow to a multicoloured neo-Gothic fantasy house which he has built systematically around an old Cornish cottage on the edge of Bodmin Moor, and in which he now lives with his wife Annie and their two children.

Perhaps wisely in view of Graham's perfectionism, they have left almost all the work on the cottage to him, Annie preferring to get on with her own art (she is a fellow Ruralist) or to arrange local social events. So Graham builds alone with frenetic attention to detail, taking time off only to paint a picture or produce another book about Victorian art or photography (he has had eight published over the last fifteen years and says another six are on the way).

It is an isolated home; even the locals are scarcely aware that it is there. You make your way down a leafy lane – very narrow with high piled banks and the trees on either side meeting in the sky above you – and abruptly come to a high concrete wall which metamorphoses into the east side of the building.

Graham points out the old corniced Cornish cottage that formed the starting point for his work. It looks like a sad little fossil embedded in the wall, dominated now by the later architectural extravaganza. The question begs to be asked: why did Graham choose to build around the cottage, rather than start afresh on clear ground?

'I would have preferred to start afresh. I probably would have chosen to build much further back from the road, but this is a green belt area and you're not allowed to do things like that. So technically Barley Splatt is an extension. It was a very ordinary little cottage before, hardly worth preserving un-altered, but I like the idea that behind the stone the cottage is still there. It provides a sense of continuity.'

There's continuity too in the name itself: it was called Barley Splatt long before Graham ever thought of moving to Cornwall, and no doubt before Graham's parents ever thought of him. Splatt is an old Cornish word for field. Graham says it will be at least twenty years before it is completed but, even in its unfinished state, Barley Splatt is an astonishing testament to his vision of the ideal house.

Inside there is more evidence that things are not completed. Some rooms, such as the kitchen, which he started first, and the gallery upstairs, are finished to perfection, with all the colours filled in, as it were; while others are no more than pencil sketches, their walls built but little else. In these rooms are piles of what looks like junk but turns out to be high-Victorian furniture. Acting as a table-tennis table in what will be the dining room, for example, is a table by Pugin.

As doors are opened on to rooms that still exist largely in Graham's imagination, you are liable to see large house spiders scuttling into their webs beneath the hinges. But from what Graham has to say about the relationship between houses and nature, I get the distinct impression that he does not resent the arachnidan intrusion. 'I wanted a richly ornamented house because man needs ornamentation around him. Nature, especially in medieval literature, isn't always pleasant. It can be a very sinister force – you've only got

PREVIOUS PAGE Barley Splatt, artist Graham Ovenden's romantic house, which he largely built himself, on the edge of Bodmin Moor in Cornwall.

BELOW *The hall stand in the kitchen was designed by Christopher Dresser.*

The gallery is furnished throughout with wallpaper and carpets designed by Pugin (OPPOSITE BELOW RIGHT), and contains a cupboard by Phillip Webb which houses a rare collection of Viennese Secession crockery (OPPOSITE BELOW LEFT) and a nude by Dod Proctor (OPPOSITE ABOVE).

LEFT *A strange mock-medieval chair at the kitchen table; most of the furniture in the house comes from Graham Ovenden's once-enormous collection, now largely sold off to pay for building the numerous 'extensions'.*

TOP *Graham Ovenden at his scullery door. The door handle is by American architect Louis Sullivan and comes from the Guarantee Building in Buffalo, New York State.*

ABOVE *The very decorative and imaginatively designed back entrance to Barley Splatt.*

to read *Sir Gawain and the Green Knight* to see that. Yet we still need it, especially today, when there is a great imbalance between man and nature.'

He is contemptuous of modern houses, in which abstract ornamentation is seldom a strong point. 'You've just got to look at most houses that have been professionally built and they're dreadful. They're brutally simple and badly made – on the principle that the more thought, time and labour involved in the building of a house the less the financial return. For a joke I had an estimate done when I first planned the house, to see how much it would cost professionally. It came to one and a quarter million pounds,' he says incredulously.

As Graham's income was hardly in that league he had to do every bit of the work himself. The original cottage, on a site of twenty-two acres which includes three-quarters of a mile of river, cost about the same as the house he sold in London, and the extensions have been built as money became available from his paintings and from books he has written.

The technical problems of building have never bothered him. 'I was one of those beasts known as child prodigies,' he explains uncompromisingly, showing me a photo of a painted harpsichord he made when he was twelve by way of illustration. He will admit that he has made a few mistakes. 'Look at the new wood around that window,' he says, pointing to a cracked and splintering frame. 'I should have used an old wood. I'm going to have to face it with a pine veneer now.'

There are enough furniture and fittings to give Barley Splatt the atmosphere of a lived-in museum: Pugin door plates identical to those put into the House of Lords (a workman probably walked off with them); a George Edmund Street stair rail in the hall; Minton tiles in the kitchen. But if it is a museum, it is one with more than a dash of medieval magic about it to bring it to life. Upstairs, the coloured window panes reflect red and green light and subtly alter the nature of the air, so a visitor catching sight of himself in a yellowing mirror will find he has an oddly Pre-Raphaelite look. And the magic will spread throughout the house as Graham continues to build his ornately decorated rooms into the surrounding countryside. Barley Splatt is becoming, as one of the Lewis Carroll characters on the wall might say, curiouser and curiouser.

MIRACLES CAN HAPPEN

Serena Allott

Photographs by James Merrell

ark Wickham's studio in Wiltshire stands between two centuries – literally. The old, rather curious low stone building looks into Devizes High Street and sits somewhat incongruously amid stationers, haberdashers and other customary shops of this bustling market town; while the back, built of brick and timber, opens on to St John's Alley, a medieval pathway.

'Several years ago, the group of buildings of which it's a part fell into the hands of a building society which wanted to turn them into a shopping mall,' says Mark. 'Luckily, three friends of mine from Marlborough bought them, but panicked when they

realized what they'd taken on.'

It was an opportune moment for Mark. Since the break-up of his marriage some years ago, he had based himself at his mother's house at Froxfield, staying with friends and borrowing houses from time to time. 'When I heard about this old Quaker meeting house, I was camping in a deserted studio in Marlborough. It was really rather rough. It seemed to be the right time to make a move and become a householder again.'

And so, a few years ago, he bought it. 'The building goes back much earlier than the Quakers, though it hasn't been dated exactly. We know they put the brick façade over the original timber structure. I suppose they wanted to make it look more imposing. Then someone – the Plymouth Brethren I think – added the panelling in the Thirties.'

Mark's Marlborough friends had not touched the place (it is a listed building) and, in spite of its having been derelict for years, it was in remarkably good condition: a back wall and staircase had to be replaced; a bathroom was needed, as was roof insulation; and the skylights in the kitchen and sitting room needed renewing.

'The council gave me a grant for all that sort of thing and, of course, I had to get planning permission to use it as a house. Apart from these necessities, and the evacuation of pigeons that were nesting on the stairs, the building is nearly as I found it. I

LEFT *Mark Wickham and Becky Herd in the sitting room dotted with his paintings and her needlework.*

ABOVE *Work in progress in the studio.*

RIGHT *A test panel for a set of giant murals for a London restaurant.*

studio and the bedroom is huge and fills the space above the studio. Cluttered with books and plants, it doubles as a sewing room for his girlfriend, Becky Herd, who is a talented needlewoman (one of her patchwork quilts adorns the bed) and as a storeroom for Mark's photographic equipment.

'My family has quite a tradition of artists,' says Mark, indicating the painting-lined walls. 'My father was a painter, photographer and cabinet-maker. He met my mother – also a painter – at the Royal Academy. And her mother, Mabel Lucie Attwell, the illustrator of children's books, was married to Harold Earnshaw, who used to illustrate for *Punch*.' The tradition goes on: Mark's younger daughter is studying ceramics at Corsham; Becky's needlework is dotted around the house; and the artistic efforts of Mark's friends add a finishing lustre a bronze bull by Richard Cowdy, a friend from art school, stands on the windowsill in the sitting room.

After the paintings, the most striking thing about the house is the number of plants, which goes some way to compensating for the lack of a garden. The kitchen, in fact, looks more like a conservatory: the plants seem to thrive in a steamy atmosphere. A shelf just below the kitchen skylight is laden with tubs full of bulbs in spring; and there are lemon and loquat trees grown from seed by a friend. 'Things have always seemed to grow of their own accord in this house. Becky helps them along – she's very good at propagating and transplanting.'

The furniture is a most haphazard collection. 'I never seem to get round to buying many things, so most of what you see here,' Mark gestures round the sitting room, 'comes from my mother's house. Of course, some of it goes back further than that – those brocade curtains, for instance, came from my grandmother's London house.' The curtains in question frame a sash window that Mark salvaged years ago from a house due for demolition. 'I pick up things like that – the fireplace surround came from the back of an old local shop, and Becky rescued that refectory table from Marlborough College. I don't honestly think I've bought a piece of furniture since I came here. I'm lucky enough to have inherited or been given or lent exactly the right amount of oddments.'

Recently, the studio has been taken over by Mark's latest project – a massive still-life mural destined for Le Champenois, a new London restaurant. It consists of thirty four-by-five-foot panels which, painted predomi-

didn't have much money, but all I really had to do was give it a coat of paint and move in.'

Mark is usually to be found with an artist's brush, not a paint roller, in his hand, so it is hardly surprising that his studio dominates the house. It is filled with the inevitable artistic clutter and, like almost all the house, is lit from above, by windows positioned just below ceiling height. Among the canvases lurk, incongruously, two modern speakers – 'for really serious listening'.

The kitchen and sitting room are lean-to, glass-roofed constructions on each side of the

nantly in pastel colours, take you through a delicately decadent gastronomic day, beginning with a breakfast of coffee and melons, and ending with post-prandial brandy and cigars. 'I don't normally paint murals,' explains Mark, 'but Le Champenois was designed by the company Wickham and Baumgarten of which my half-brother Julyan is a partner. He had been looking for an opportunity for us to work together for ages, so he asked me to do this.'

As for the style of Mark's work, the composition is calculatedly simple, the detail painstakingly elaborate and the overall impression one of airy crispness. At the Slade he developed a technique influenced, he claims, by Bellini, Cézanne, Morandi, the French Post-Impressionists and – to a certain extent – David Hockney. Then two or three years ago his interest switched to painting portraits. 'I enjoy the challenge of making people appear as they actually are. As most of my subjects are very busy I tend to go to them, which has its disadvantages: often there's very little light and space, the telephone rings constantly and children run in and out. But

at least you get people in their own surroundings.'

After the initial sittings, Mark returns to his studio and works from photographs, finally producing paintings so detailed that they can take two years to complete, which means two years of agony as well as ecstasy. 'When I have problems I wish my studio wasn't the hub of the house. It means Becky is affected by my moods. So I often change the house round in the summer and work in the sitting room, which makes quite a good studio because of the huge skylight.'

Many of Mark's subjects are famous people, but he displays very little of his work and hates having to hassle with London dealers, 'partly because I'm rather frightened of laying myself open to serious criticism'. Besides, he very much appreciates his privacy. Although he has lived in the Marlborough area for years, he delights in the fact that in Devizes he knows almost no one.

'It suits me to keep a low profile while I'm working. It's such a wonderfully anonymous sort of house from the outside – not many of the locals even know I'm here.'

LEFT *The studio, formerly the meeting hall, dominates the house.*

OPPOSITE *Jasmine and a vine transform the kitchen into a conservatory.*

UNDISCOVERED COUNTRY

Despite the advent of the car and of high-speed trains, the increase in tourism and decentralization, there remain many unspoiled and almost forgotten corners of the British Isles. Often only a short distance from towns that throb with foreign visitors are tracts of land that have been unchanged for hundreds of years, although upheavals in farming mean that prairie-type fields have long since replaced hedged smallholdings ploughed by tenant farmers.

Everyone has a favourite place, somewhere to go and reflect away from the din of everyday life, or a place which is full of childhood memories, like Maggie Gee's Isle of Purbeck. The Cotswolds are one of Britain's most popular tourist attractions, and yet even there, once away from the seething show villages of Stow, Bourton-on-the-Water and Broadway, are tiny hamlets inhabited by people who own cottages lived in by their ancestors from time immemorial.

Living on an island, as we do, the sea is never far away and is a rich and important seam in our national consciousness. Long stretches of our coastline have remained untouched as Winston Graham discovers in the surf-washed bays just south of Newquay in Cornwall. Even more remote is the wild beauty of the Yorkshire Dales which James Herriot has loved for nearly half a century.

It is a delight to know just how much of our country we have still failed to destroy.

OPPOSITE *A view across the fertile farmland of the Isle of Purbeck in Dorset towards Kimmeridge Bay.*

OF CORNISH COVES AND CLIFFS

Winston Graham

Photographs by Simon McBride

My association with Cornwall can be divided into three phases. The first might be called the phase of delighted discovery; the second that of sun and sea addiction; the third that of nostalgic return.

The phase of 'delighted discovery' must have lasted eight or nine years; it coincided with my earliest writing years. There was always somewhere new to go, or somewhere familiar to us but new to our friends who came in the summer. I grew to take a sort of proprietary pleasure, not only in the beauty of coves and cliffs but in the legends and the history of Cornwall.

The vegetation of the north Cornish coast could hardly have been more different from Manchester where I was born and bred. Trees – there were hardly any trees at all as I knew them. Nothing, of course, near the sea. Even valleys such as Perrancombe could only boast a few wind-tortured elms. But the under-growth was altogether different. This rampaged and flourished everywhere. The hedges, the verges, the commons, the railway banks, were choked with weeds, which in their season became wild flowers. In the spring, campion and milkmaids and bluebells fought with each other in patriotic colour, disputing their ground with fern and bracken and gorse and cow parsnip and wild garlic and a dozen other rivals for a place in the rain and the sun. Some years the colour of the gorse would be so outrageous as to hurt the eye.

In undeveloped land near my mother's bungalow where I first lived a tin stamp still worked, fed by a leat which was a diversion from the stream that ran at the foot of our garden. The water passed *above* our bungalow on the other side of the road and, a hundred yards further on, it ran under the road and was allowed to fall over a water-wheel, and so activate the iron crushing heads that broke up the ore tipped here from a nearby mine. The water then worked two circular washing floors before rejoining the main stream.

After I was married this piece of land came up for sale, and, so that no one should build next to the bungalow, I bought it. By now the stamps were a ruin, the wheels aslant, the iron rods rusty and long silent. One day a young man with a dark complexion and a pointed beard called on me and asked me if I owned the 'stamps land' up Perrancombe, and, by association, the stamps. I said I did. He explained that he was operating a small tin mine on his own and that parts of the wheel and the heads and lifters would be useful to him. Could he buy them? As there was no prospect of my making use of them, I agreed that he could have them, and at no cost to himself except the transport. He was pleased at this and we chatted a few minutes in the autumn sunshine. He was upset at the way Cornwall was getting spoiled, and felt it was largely the result of up-country folk coming to the county and developing it for their own profit. He also expressed a grudge against up-country writers who came here and wrote about the county and made money out of it all. Interested in this remark, I asked him if he had any particular writers in mind. He replied: 'Well, this chap Winston Graham, for instance.'

I blurted out my guilt at once. He did not see this as amusing, but neither was he at all embarrassed. After a few seconds of thought-ful staring he explained accusatively that he lived at Mingoose, and that since the early *Poldark* novels were published he had been much troubled by people coming around looking for Mingoose House, where in the novels the Treneglos family lives. 'They come round my place Sat'day af'noons, Sunday mornings. Tis a proper nuisance!' After I had apologised again for being who I was, how-ever, he came to take a more favourable view of me. Had I ever been down a one-man mine? No, I said. 'Then come Sunday af'noon, I'll show'ee.' Which he did. It was clearly part of an old mine which he had redeveloped. The ladders where shaky and so in the end was I. Later we went back to his cottage for tea, and he played me hymn tunes on the organ he had himself built into the wall of the cottage. A character – and Cornwall is rich in characters.

Cornish sunshine has one of the highest tanning capacities in the world. You can get browner during a week here than during three in Nice. People account for this by speaking of the wind, but it is probably more than that; the air is so light that ultraviolet rays pass through it more intensely. But, of course, to go with the sun there has to be sea. Without it the sun is oppressive, headachy, tiring. With the close proximity of the sea all that is changed.

One year, the evening before my son went to his public school, we escaped on to Perran-porth beach on an incoming tide. There was no wind and the sun was hot but it was a huge sea. It was one of those seas when a surfer catches one wave, is borne along a dizzying way, then dropped upon another, and so upon another, and even sometimes on a fourth. As we staggered together out of the sea joyfully exhausted after our fifteenth such run, my son said to me: 'Daddy, people who have never done this haven't lived.' I believe he was not far wrong.

West Pentire was the beach to which we went most often. Here the surf is chancy – you have to pick and choose your time to

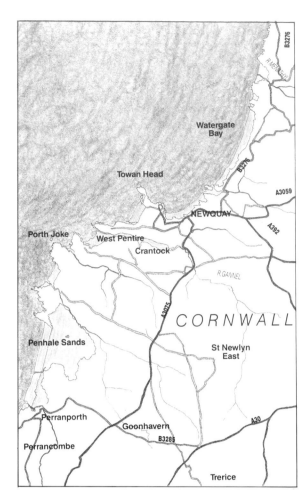

ABOVE LEFT
Winston Graham in front of Wheal Bush Mine, Todpool, one of the many deserted tin mines characteristic of the Cornish landscape.

LEFT *The coastal path at West Pentire.*

PAGE 124 *Perranporth Bay, one of the surf-washed bays on the north Cornish coast.*

catch it – but a narrow cove there offers the perfect suntrap and is protected from everything except a south-east wind. It is a fine beach at low tide and the cove forms a rock-fringed swimming pool when the tide comes in. Other smaller pools, refilled each tide, are constantly fished by small boys and their fathers during the summer months, and thin white legs stalk and paddle in and out of the water, examining the sea anemones, the crabs, and the fishes built like spectral shrimps which dart in and out of the gently waving weed. Northerly winds may whistle overhead and make the rest of the county shiver – but this cove is protected from them. Sometimes, and not infrequently, you bask in drowsy sun while monumental clouds hover over the rest of Cornwall. It is a charmed spot. It was this cove, and the headland that juts out beyond it making the western claw of Crantock Bay, and the further bay beyond of Porth Joke – or Polly Joke, as it is known locally – which helped most to make up a picture of the Nampara of the *Poldark* novels.

It was West Pentire where I spent so much of my time; watching the flickering colours in the water, the white flash of gulls' wings, angular and sharp, against slanting skies; the sea pinks clinging perpendicularly to the gentler rocks like close-cropped pink beards; the thump of waves forcing their way through a blowhole and turning spume into mist; the welter of wildflowers in the unspoiled fields; the flat almost slaty rocks that slid quietly by steps into the sea at the point's end; the endless procession of cloud and sun against the background of the wide skies.

It was here I walked often with the girl I was going to marry, threshing through the low surf a mile across the beach and back, planning our honeymoon – which never came off because of the outbreak of war. Five years later we returned, and picked and hacked our way down the overgrown paths, slashing at nettles and brambles, and negotiating as best we could the fences of barbed wire, reaching at last our beloved cove. It was untouched, unchanged: there might have been no war, no bloodshed, no terror, no hatred, no torture, no genocide, no Belsens, no Stalingrads, no Hiroshimas. The sea was just creeping round the corner of the cove, a ripple advancing over the dry sand, retreating again as if not sure. A large herring gull, feet planted primly on a nearby rock, eyed us askance. He had become unused to such intrusion.

We had returned. We have been returning ever since.

ABOVE The tiny secure inlet of Porth Joke, known as Polly Joke by the local people.

Trerice Manor, a small Elizabethan house, was Winston Graham's model for Trenwith, the home of the Poldarks.

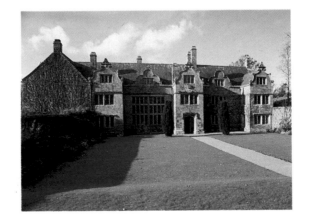

THE ISLE OF PURBECK

Maggie Gee

Photographs by Ian Howes

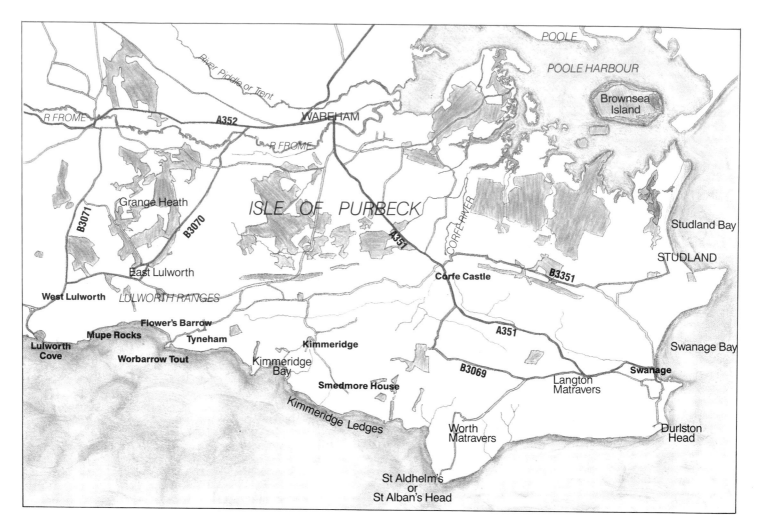

'There are people who were born in Poole or Bournemouth who have never visited the Isle of Purbeck,' says Damaris Mansel, owner of one of Purbeck's most beautiful manor houses, Smedmore. 'There are people born in this village who have never crossed over Wareham Bridge,' says a Purbeck girl who sees the other side of the coin.

A Victorian history of the Isle of Purbeck explains why it is so delightfully underpopulated. The 'island' was 'originally, like the New Forest, a wild hunting ground of our Norman and probably even Saxon kings... The first requisite of a ... warren is that it should be kept in a wild, half peopled, untilled state; and in such a condition for ages were successive kings able to keep the Isle of Purbeck, much assisted by the barriers of heath, hill and water which divide it from the rest of Dorsetshire'.

For the first thirty-five years of my life Dorset meant my birthplace – I left Poole behind when I was three. In 1984 I went back to find my origins and wandered beyond them, west of Swanage, to discover the

strange, steep, largely unspoiled country of the Isle of Purbeck. It is mainly farming country, with just a few small-scale industries like stone quarrying and clay mining. Tourism is still almost exclusively a summer industry; and even then, you can take long unhurried walks over the hills around Corfe Castle and along the breathtaking coastal path between Swanage and Flower's Barrow, without seeing more than a few black insect people in the distance struggling up the slopes. The winds blow hard along this path, especially in winter. The grass is short, tough and sheep-coloured and the trees show the wiry strength of their wind-carved skeletons.

Drama of outline is commonplace. The cliffs dip and soar so that a clifftop 'walk' quickly turns into a climb, one step at a time, up rough single footholds cut into the turf, the horizon canted forty-five degrees in front of you. At Worbarrow Tout and Mupe Rocks, exposed layers of rock, regular but tipped at a crazy angle to the level of the sea, thrust their way skywards. The ruined grandeur of Corfe Castle astonishes as you turn a curve in the road and see it way above you on a high round

PREVIOUS PAGE *The spectacular cliff walk at St Aldhelm's (or St Alban's) Head.*

hill, breaking into the sunset like a fierce row of teeth, light whistling straight through the gaps in the old masonry. An awe-inspiring sight indeed.

The castle is magnificent, but it is only a shell. Practical local people built the village called Corfe Castle out of the stone remains of the castle itself, blown up during the Civil War. Sheep – when I was there last, one black renegade browsed a little apart from all the others – now graze the sides of the castle mound. The gradient seems about to tip them brusquely off on to the road below. Like those of many of the other local villages, the cottages of Corfe Castle are built and roofed with yellow-grey Purbeck stone and fronted by bright flowerbeds. In summer this village is far from undiscovered, but in spring it is much quieter and you can think yourself in another century. You can also stay in a renovated Elizabethan manor house, Moretons House Hotel, built in the shape of an E as a tribute to Elizabeth I, with attractive, E-shaped walled gardens.

Corfe Castle is the ideal base from which to visit the part of Purbeck which interests me most, the Lulworth Ranges. Here, the royal huntsmen who once preserved the landscape in its wild state have been succeeded by an even more effective barrier against modern development – the army. The Ranges stretch between Kimmeridge Bay and Lulworth Cove – both villages are just outside them. The army now occupies over a thousand acres of Purbeck's most striking scenery. After public protest, they have opened up the Ranges to the public every weekend of the year and for two complete months in summer. What you find as you drive or walk past the large signs – 'Open today' – is a country untouched by intensive agriculture, modern building developments or large through roads. Small roads and well-marked footpaths lead you across rolling hills into valleys like Tyneham Valley, and then the land sweeps up steeply again to spectacular coastal formations like Gad Cliff where

cormorants can be seen wheeling around the sheer limestone.

Tyneham is a unique place, a ghost village now, its houses roofless: both beautiful and tragic. In 1943 this little fishing village, set quite alone in a valley leading down to Worbarrow Bay, was evacuated and taken over by the army – the manor house, dating back to the fourteenth century, was occupied by the Women's Auxiliary Air Force (WAAF) and is remembered affectionately by at least one of them. The villagers were given a written promise '. . . you have every right to return to the property'. They left at short notice, pinning a note to the church door: 'We have given up our homes, where many of us have lived for generations, to help win the war to keep men free. We shall return one day and thank you for treating the village kindly.'

But they were never allowed to come back. The cottages slowly deteriorated with gunnery practice and manoeuvres until, in the end, the roofs were removed and the walls capped. When I last visited it, historical irony was rampant. Driving into the village I could not believe my eyes: there was thatch on the cottages again, and panes in the windows, But to my astonishment a little further on a 'stone' facing on a house was visibly peeling away – it was just plastic. A film company was using the village for a film about that other group of gallant Dorset exiles – commonly believed to be founders of trade unionism in England – the Tolpuddle Martyrs.

A major campaign in 1972 for Tyneham to be returned to its villagers nearly succeeded – but, alas, most of the original inhabitants were either dead or had settled elsewhere and the pre-war paradise remembered in Lilian Bond's *Tyneham: A Lost Heritage* could never be re-created.

Paradoxically, the Lulworth Ranges have become a kind of ecological paradise, with a snake or two. At Arish Mell I once saw a tank still burning fiercely from the previous day's exercise. But, for the most part, the Ranges are a haven for all kinds of plants, birds and butterflies that have dwindled elsewhere because of pesticides, the motor car or other similarly destructive products of modern life. Nature is good at adapting to the more obvious kinds of damage army manoeuvres do; shell holes have become pools where dragonflies breed. There are more butterflies here than I have seen anywhere else in England in the summer. Marbled whites, male blues, and tawny Lulworth skippers dance in clouds near the cliff edge. The sheep

LEFT FROM THE TOP
Corfe Castle, once a magnificent stronghold, was destroyed by the Parliamentarians after a lengthy siege during the Civil War; productive farmland extends over much of the Isle of Purbeck; Kimmeridge Bay, which is now the home of the Purbeck Marine Wildlife Reserve; the Norman chapel at St Aldhelm's Head.

graze turf thick with clover, bird's-foot trefoil, vetch and vivid blue viper's bugloss. You can still see cowslips, and harebells, even the occasional orchid – and a skylark will suddenly sing high above you. Former hedges have thickened into long dark coppices, sprawling down the pale grassland like sleeping animals.

The need for an animal welfare organization at Church Knowle, however, is a reminder of modern-day life in the surrounding areas of Dorset. The Margaret Green Foundation Trust rescues local waifs and strays – ponies, donkeys, rabbits, cats and dogs – then takes on the task of finding new homes for them all.

This is walking country. The roads are so narrow that cars slow to pass abreast. No road runs within a mile of the sea – except at Kimmeridge, where you can drive right down to the strange black bay, which is now the home of the Purbeck Marine Wildlife Reserve, and see corn-marigolds, hairy buttercups or sea pinks on the edge of the low cliffs.

Enjoy it while you can. The Ranges themselves will not succumb to development while the army is there, but Purbeck is mineral-rich land. Early attempts to develop the mineral wealth were only partially successful: Kimmeridge villagers tried to sell their black bituminous shale, Kimmeridge Coal, as fuel to make lamp oil, but the sulphurous smell you can faintly detect near the clifftop puts the public off. Now, however, a major oil field has been discovered at Wytch Farm, not far from Corfe Castle, and another very recently in Poole Harbour on the north-eastern edge of Purbeck. High oil prices in the future could mean changes. Inevitably there would be more traffic and more people would get to know about the lovely, desolate landscape of the Ranges and their summer transformation into a dense mosaic of wild flowers.

At Tyneham, only the church has been fully preserved in its original state – minus the congregation. There is a particularly beautiful twentieth-century memorial window, inserted before the war that would change much of rural England for good and, at the same time, stop Tyneham and the surrounding country in its tracks curiously outside history. In the lateral panes of the window, the artist has included a scattering of local butterflies in his pattern; they still fly on in the unused church with the sun pouring through them, trapped in human memory above the stained-glass fishing boats and the ghosts of Tyneham's fishermen.

RIGHT FROM THE TOP
The coastguard station at St Aldhelm's Head; the striking coastal feature of Lulworth Cove; the combination of lush farmland and breathtaking coastal scenery from St Aldhelm's Head; typical Purbeck stone cottages in the picturesque village of Worth Matravers.

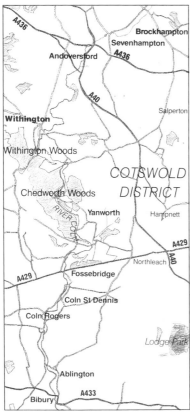

THE WILD WOLDS

Vanessa Berridge

Photographs by Roy A. Giles

ABOVE *The view from Yanworth over the Chedworth Woods is one of the finest in the North Cotswolds.*

OPPOSITE ABOVE *Brockhampton Park is a rambling fusion of sixteenth- and nineteenth-century architecture.*

OPPOSITE BELOW *The simple Norman church at Winson, behind which stands an austerely classical mansion.*

Gloucestershire is scarcely an unsung county: its famous show villages of Bourton-on-the-Water, Stow-on-the-Wold, Broadway and Bibury feature in every guidebook and seethe with tourists in spring, summer and autumn. The mass migration of the royals to the area has increased its popularity and ensured that the paparazzi are never far away.

But Gloucestershire's true charm lies in its hidden corners, of which there are still many. It is, in effect, two very different counties. The South Cotswolds, where the royals have set up home, feature snug, tree-lined slopes; this is Laurie Lee country and the snow settles deep in winter, but it is more sheltered and welcoming than the barren escarpment of the North Cotswolds. Here, the wind has a cutting force and when I return from London I am always struck by the chill calm and beauty of these hills – fiercely green in summer and gloriously golden in autumn. Above all, these hills are quiet. In Brockhampton, where I lived for ten happy years, a 'foreigner's' car is a rare sight.

Nestling comfortably in a hollow, Bibury marks the transition between the two faces of the county. Through the village, with its ever-present ice cream vendors, bubbles the River Coln, as busy by then as Bibury itself. As you follow the shrinking river's course back up to its source above Brockhampton, the landscape changes noticeably, opening out with hedgeless fields spread below broad skies and racing clouds. The horizon light is sharper, almost bleak. This is a land of contrasts: the paler green of the fields, water meadows and deciduous trees throw into sharp relief the threateningly dark evergreens of Chedworth and Withington Woods. These woods seem to encroach upon the nearby villages, which huddle for safety around their churches and tiny village greens. Some are braver, such as Ablington and Yanworth, stretching out nonchalantly along the lanes with little or no centre. Daringly, Yanworth's twelfth-century church stands a little way from the village, surrounded by large barns and seeming part of a farmyard.

The villages along the northern reaches of the Coln are insular, set apart apparently from the mainstream of contemporary life,

and, televisions aside, the villagers lead lives very little different from those of their ancestors. It takes time to be accepted: I was held to be a foreigner for most of the time I lived in Brockhampton and when I returned to work in London, the villagers knew they had always been right. The communities in villages such as these are tight-knit, the main event of the year being the Produce Show in September. The same people are expected to win each year with their jumbo carrots, onions and marrows and perfectly spherical potatoes. A newcomer may be lucky enough to be awarded third prize for her pâté, but she cannot hope to win anything again for another twenty years. The same families have dominated the villages for generations and horizons are as narrow as the skies are wide. My mother once asked a villager whether she had always lived in the area. 'Oh no,' she replied, 'I was born in Guiting Power' (all of

three miles away).

The joy of this valley is the ease with which you can escape and wander alone. Walk or drive just two miles up the road from Bibury and you will find yourself in Ablington, unchanged for centuries and its little street deserted. A stroll along the winding lanes is as pleasant as a walk across the fields, but no farmer will stop you crossing his land so long as you shut the gate and do not chase the sheep. The villages themselves vary in wealth and distinction – both Withington and Ablington have more than their fair share of fine houses, many of them inhabited by wealthy newcomers rather than natives of the county.

Ablington's imposing houses stand well back from the road, shielded by high walls and immaculate hedges. Ablington House, built in about 1650, has stone lions from the Houses of Parliament on its gateposts, gazing

ABOVE *Halewell Close was a small monastery in the fourteenth century. When Elizabeth Carey-Wilson* (OPPOSITE BELOW) *bought it in 1971 it was a ramshackle collection of farmhouses, cottages and barns. Having renovated the buildings she now runs the house as a small hotel.*

The main building at the Mill Inn at Withington, a beautiful Cotswold stone pub, is over five hundred years old.

haughtily out across the Coln. On the occasional day in summer, luxuriant gardens are opened to the public for such worthy charities as the Distressed Gentlefolk's Association. It is these houses, too, that are more than likely to host the AGM and cocktail parties of the local Conservatives.

Villages such as Brockhampton and Yanworth are less distinguished architecturally, but both command magnificent views. Yanworth looks out over Chedworth Woods, while Brockhampton, straggling up its long hill, has a panorama of half Gloucestershire, a patchwork of fields, trees, lanes and sky, all reflecting every gradual change of season.

Cotswold architecture has a very distinctive character. Despite chill winds that blow along the Coln valley, all its villages have a welcoming warmth about them. Their great houses more closely resemble the cottages by which they are surrounded than houses of the

same period elsewhere. They are, in fact, more like extended cottages themselves. For example, the Glebe House at Coln Rogers and Brockhampton Park are both rambling fusions of sixteenth- and nineteenth-century architecture. The manor house at Cassey Compton, a mile east of Withington, is a typical example of how Cotswold builders modified classicism, grafting on a special timeless quality. It is rare, and surprising, to come across a mansion such as that at Winson which is austerely classical.

These rambling, yellow-grey houses are, to me, one of the chief delights of this little-explored valley. Indeed, for both natural and manmade beauty, it has much to offer. From Bibury to Brockhampton, there is scarcely a shop to be seen (although there are a number of good pubs, including the 500-year-old Mill Inn at Withington), so its quiet is almost undisturbed, a welcome relief for any visitor.

ON TOP OF THE WORLD

James Herriot

Photographs by Derry Brabbs

Though I love all the dales, it is in Coverdale that I have spent my holidays. To be exact, in the tiny village of West Scrafton. The word Scrafton means the 'town by the hollow' and the village is a closely packed group of ancient houses around the smallest green I have ever seen.

We stayed in Grange Cottage, rented from the then owner Dr Ralph Dubberley. It is a characterful old house with the green on one side and a deep gill and beck on the other. It was originally one of the granges of the monks of Coverham Abbey and has a magnificent fifteenth-century window stretching from the kitchen into the main bedroom, giving an unusually ecclesiastical look to both rooms. It also means that every word spoken in the kitchen can be heard upstairs.

You have only to walk out of the door and look up at the long rocky comb on the crest of Roova Crag to feel you have found somewhere exciting. The crag overhangs the village from a height of over 1,500 feet and it is the pleasantest of strolls to follow the track to the summit, then along to the old mine workings and come back to the village via the beck with its hidden pools and falls which are seen only by the farmers and shepherds. I spent many autumn afternoons up on the crag with my dogs, either wandering over the mounds and tussocks or stretched out on the crisp grass, looking at the grey blanket of fog rolling over the plain below. Down there it would be dank and dark, but on the crag it was a glittering world of sun and blue skies with the peace and silence wrapping me round.

On one side, above the stone walls, rose the crag, leading in a noble ridge over the Great Haw, Carle Fell and Little Whernside, and on the other the land dipped to the floor of the dale with the steep slopes rising to Penhill and Carlton Moor. The long village of Carlton was like a drawn-out grey thread against the green.

Coverdale is, in a sense, a hidden place. It doesn't open up at its foot and beckon you in as do Swaledale and Wensleydale. You have to seek it out. Among the softness and gentle green banks of Middleham Low Moor, you would not suspect that just round the corner a secluded valley led between steep bare hills for twelve miles into some of the bleakest country in England. It is beautiful, but it is a stark beauty of treeless heights and squat grey houses except at its foot around Coverham Bridge and the Abbey ruins, where the more amiable surroundings are a delight.

Since we were catering for ourselves, we had to buy provisions regularly and the food shops were abundant and excellent. Even in lonely Carlton there was an excellent store and when I saw their selection, I thought of the days when I was in my twenties and felt lucky to be able to buy a digestive biscuit and

a slice of Wensleydale cheese to sustain me on my rounds. Middleham, too, is splendidly supplied, while Leyburn is a positive revelation. That windswept little town on the hillside can fix you up with everything you want from groceries, home-baked pastries and butcher meat to wearing apparel for both sexes.

Of course, I spent most of the time roaming among the fells with an Ordnance Survey map tucked in my anorak. It may not sound very exciting to follow those lines of dots which cross the contours of the hillsides, but in Coverdale I found it a continual thrill. especially when my peregrinations took me to the wild country at the dale head.

I recall one day among that awesome vastness when I had the wonderful feeling of being on the roof of England. Gazing at the

PREVIOUS PAGE *The stark beauty of Coverdale, a landscape of steep bare hills and grey stone houses.*

LEFT *Grange Cottage in West Scrafton where the Herriots spent many family holidays.*

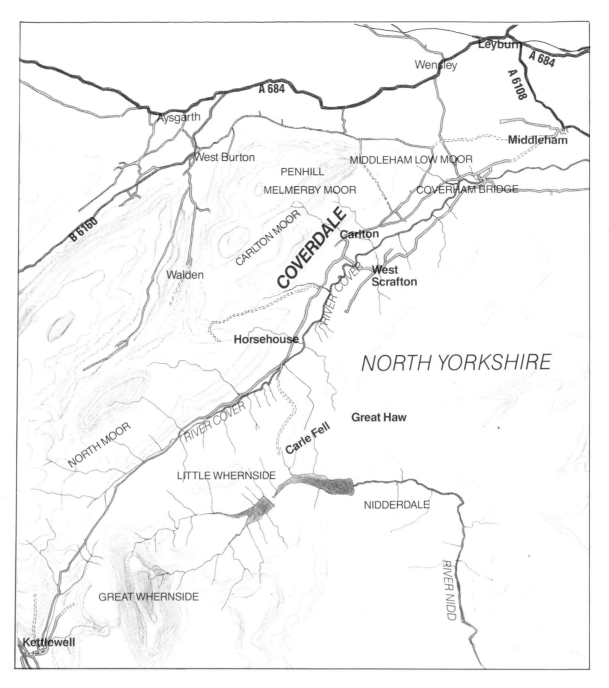

ABOVE *One of the tiny gills feeding into the River Cover, which gives the region its name.*

enormous grass-clad bulk of Great Whernside, I looked over to where the whole landscape falls away to Wharfedale and at the flanks of the great fell where countless centuries had carved out the gullies where unseen streams played and secret waterfalls splashed among their rocks.

All around, the sweet smell of the miles of moorland grass and the silence, complete except for the distant bleating of a sheep. And the sensation, which is comforting at times, of being quite alone; there was no living creature in sight – just me and my dogs.

The River Cover has its beginning up here and I could see it coiling its way with little flashes of silver towards the softer country below, bubbling under humpbacked bridges, between towering slopes with the patches of dead bracken almost scarlet against the

yellowed grass.

The jewel of the whole dale is Middleham itself, unequalled for its sheer volume of historical associations. Nowadays its soul is in the many racing stables around it. The stable lads with their hands thrust into their breeches pockets as they come in for a pint of beer would laugh if I said Middleham was a glamorous place, but it is to me.

There is much to say about Coverdale which is not apparent on the surface and I suppose most people would conclude that Coverdale's greatest wonder is the long story of the medieval eminence of Middleham, the blazing pageantry and pomp which once echoed among the grey stones and cobbles of the quiet town.

But to me Coverdale is wonderful because of its austere beauty.

A RUGGED PATH
ALONG THE PENNINES

Lesley Howes

Photographs by
Ian and Lesley Howes

The walk offers dramatic views across the Pennine landscape, which is punctuated by derelict farms.

Sometimes camping and sometimes staying at inns, we set out with sleeping bags, rucksacks, a camp stove, a tent, and a substantial amount of optimism. The weather, we assured ourselves, would soon clear up and when it did we would ramble across open moorland enjoying the view. As it turned out, it was one of the wettest months on record. The tent was washed away one night, and our boots shrank as we squelched our way through sodden peatbogs. But the scenery was spectacular, even through sheets of rain; when the sun did shine it was a bonus.

Many people walk the Pennine Way, but increasingly nowadays they force march along the crags with a neurotic desire to get to their destination as quickly as possible. This is a pity – by going about it this way, they completely miss out on the staggering beauty of a journey that most people do only once in a lifetime. The average walker goes northwards, starting from the village of Edale in the Peak District, and, if he does the whole route, walks the 270 miles up to Kirk Yetholm in Scotland. But we broke with this tradition. Being Cumbrians – by choice if not by birth – we felt we were already near the top. So we decided to start from our house and proceed southwards towards the usual starting point of Edale.

As any seasoned Cumbrian well knows, the Pennine Way must be treated with respect.

You cannot enjoy its bleak and wild beauty without crossing some very rugged country. Up there, the whims of British weather can become extremely serious. So we had equipped ourselves properly, and had done several practice walks, using these experiments to find out how much we could comfortably carry. Suitably prepared, we set off.

From our house it is a 2,000-foot climb to the top of Cross Fell, along the old 'corpse road' where, several centuries before, funeral processions had to bring bodies over the hills by packhorse from Garrigill to the nearest consecrated ground in Kirkland. At 2,930 feet, Cross Fell is the highest point of the Pennine Way. The Helm wind, a natural phenomenon resulting from the funnelling effect of the surrounding fells, can roar non-stop for days. Here, on the very top of the Pennines, is a land of rolling fells, cotton grass, peat and curlews. On a clear day you can see as far as Scotland and even coast to coast, according to some. Cross Fell is also the source of the Tees, one of the country's wildest rivers.

From this point we turned south over Great Dun Fell and Little Dun Fell and down into Dufton, our destination that night. Dufton, a small cluster of sandstone cottages, some lime-washed, and a pub, is arranged round a village green complete with trees – a very welcome sight after the bleak uplands.

The next landmark, High Cup Nick, is a

horseshoe-shaped valley, its upper edge rimmed with eighty-foot cliffs. From the top, the view stretches beyond the valley floor, and on across the Eden Valley to the Lake District peaks beyond.

From sweeping views we moved on across peat bogs to a piece of local history. Moss Shop is a tumbledown enclosure near a derelict lead mine. 'Shop' was the local word for the hillside shelters where miners stayed during their working week when these high fells were exploited for lead. After its heyday in the nineteenth century, lead mining here largely died out, with now only the occasional shaft or spoil heap as a reminder.

At Cauldron Snout, the Tees is set free again from Cow Green Reservoir. During our wet weather walk, it crashed in a raging froth at this spot, 150 feet down a natural staircase, the sides damp with spray. The Pennine Way descends alongside the torrent, and past the escarpment of Falcon Clints where peregrines still fly. Following the river to Widdybank Farm, we found a welcome sign bearing the legend *Teas*.

The five miles from nearby High Force, the biggest waterfall in England, to Middleton in Teesdale, is a pretty walk even in the rain – in contrast to the prevailing bleakness, softer and greener. It winds along the Tees through broad meadows of wild flowers and countless rabbits, cutting its way through a green valley lined with neat whitewashed farms. Middleton itself is a large grey village built in the last century by the London Lead Company, a Quaker firm which constructed houses, schools and chapels. As well as opening new mines, the firm laid roads into the hills, most of which are now grassy tracks.

From the Tees, we climbed back on to the hills, crossing open moorland to Goldsborough, a millstone outcrop rising from a peat bog and – beyond this – West Loups, a tumbledown farm surrounded by barbed wire and forbidding signs erected by the Ministry of Defence declaring it a training area. If the steady rain was not enough, a barbed wire fence hung with *Danger – Keep Out* notices dramatically lowered our spirits. But there was worse to come. A mile or two further on, the skyline was dominated by skeletons of long-abandoned military huts, and here the signs were even more sinister: *Danger, Poison Gas, Keep Out*. It was a relief to reach the village of Bowes and stroll past the Norman watchtower and Dotheboys Hall of *Nicholas Nickleby* fame.

Walking on to Tan Hill, we were back on a

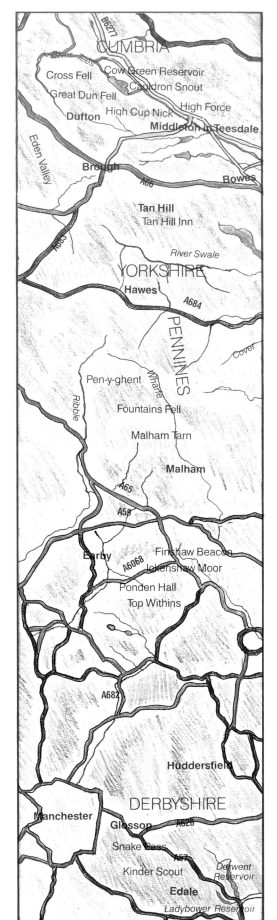

wilderness of high moors, peat bogs and hill farms. But the drenched bogs and driving rain forced us, alas, on to a road. Boots, it seems, can shrink if immersed for two whole days in mud and peat: our first blisters had just appeared. Emerging from fog, we stayed at Tan Hill Inn, the highest inn in England, and drank beer before an open fire.

In rain and mist the following day we took the wrong path and followed the River Swale through its upper dale, a chessboard of stone walls framing neat little fields, many with stone barns knowns as 'laithes'. We regained the Pennine Way by road.

The Pennine Way climbs steeply up a Roman road from the market town of Hawes to join the Dales Way, an old packhorse route along a pleasant high-level walk with views of Pen-y-ghent on one side and distant glimpses of the Carlisle–Settle railway's magnificent

viaducts on the other. The panoramic views from the 2,273-foot Pen-y-ghent make it a vital landmark, but the best time for a visit is apparently April: the summit is ablaze with purple mountain saxifrage, and the sweet wrappers left by the previous summer's country lovers have been tidied away by Nature.

Descending a natural stairway, we noticed a transition from gritstone to limestone, both underfoot and on the drystone walls. Almost immediately we climbed again, this time to the vast undulating Fountains Fell at over 2,000 feet, the site of ancient coal mines. The way dropped slightly down to Malham Tarn, a stretch of water surprisingly abundant in wildlife for its position, 1,300 feet above sea level: beside it is the imposing mansion, Malham Tarn House.

Both this house and the tarn are now the property of the National Trust, and used as a field-study centre. Built in the last century, the house has seen such famous visitors as Charles Dickens, John Ruskin and Charles Kingsley. It was here that Kingsley found the

inspiration for his famous children's book, *The Water Babies*. Kingsley's Lowthwaite Crag is Malham Cove, where today young climbers display their skills; but we reach the top via man-made steps.

Shaped like a huge amphitheatre, it overlooks the scattered stone houses of Malham village below, famous for the Buck Inn whose hiker's bar serves homemade steak and kidney pie and Theakston's bitter from the wood.

The southward path becomes gentler, a riverside walk through rolling farmland to a double arched bridge, one atop the other, with carries the A59 over the Leeds and Liverpool canal. We followed the canal for some distance at a pace only slightly slower than the brightly coloured narrowboats which carry tourists along this once busy route.

A pleasant walk through well grazed pastures and low green hills took us past Pinhaw Beacon and over Ickenshaw Moor with its incongruous pre-war holiday chalets. Then down into Brontë country. We stopped overnight at Ponden Hall, the Thrushcross Grange of *Wuthering Heights*. The nostalgia here was not so much for the Brontës' world as for the Sixties – the place is run by people best described as time-warp hippies. They created such a relaxed and pleasant atmosphere that we were reluctant to leave. The path goes on up through cotton grass and heather to a disappointingly ordinary ruin called Top Withins, thought to be the model for *Wuthering Heights*.

The weather changed dramatically for the worse, and with clothes and packs soaked, we opted for public transport to rejoin the Way from Glossop, climbing up on to the Snake Pass in Derbyshire. Our troubles were not over: ahead was a sea of black peat sludge called Featherbed Moss. Here the cavalry charge of Pennine Way starters has etched a broad path across the slopes.

It all became worthwhile again, however, as we crossed onto Kinder Scout and picked our way over wind-carved gritstone to the end of the journey. There, above the village of Edale, we stood on moorland which was once the exclusive preserve of grouse shooters. It could have remained private land for the amusement of a few – but in 1932 some 400 walkers made a mass trespass. Although some were jailed, their efforts led to long negotiations which eventually allowed the opening in 1965 of the English leg of Britain's first great footpath.

OPPOSITE *Malham Cove, a three-hundred-foot cliff above Malham village.*

BELOW *Lesley Howes tackles the steep hill leading out of Hawes.*

COUNTRY LIFESTYLES

Another great cliché, of course, is that if you scratch an Englishman you will find a country dweller. Cities are not our natural habitat – we have never been a nation of city states as were Italy and Germany.

Fresh air and fields are our ideal, our preferred environment the narrow horizons of a small country village. Those who are obliged to live in cities for their jobs either dream of a second home in the country or hope that they may eventually be able to move out to provide a better place for their children to grow up in.

Writers and artists are in the enviable position of frequently being able to ply their trade wherever they choose. Several of the country dwellers featured here are such people, lucky and brave enough to make the break. Mathew Spender, son of the poet Stephen, has gone a stage further and has made his home in that most English of foreign retreats – Tuscany – where many of his artist friends and colleagues are also expatriates.

Others have moved their businesses to the country, where they find they are now flourishing. The intriguing mix of lifestyles, and their shared enjoyment, must surely encourage all those who would like to find their perfect country retreat.

OPPOSITE *The lush landscape of Dorset surrounds the village where Lady Rachel Billington and her family have chosen to make their home.*

GOING IT ALONE

Kate Corbett-Winder

Photographs by Timothy Beddow

Camping in a derelict barn on top of a windswept Welsh mountain is not everyone's idea of a honeymoon. For Roderick and Gillie James it was the start of building a life and their first home together. For eighteen months they worked like pioneers in a strange country, restoring a barn that had been uninhabited, except by cows, for nearly seventy years.

Today the Jameses live in a different barn. It is a seventeenth-century bakery on the edge of a Cotswold village, where they moved a few years ago with their first two sons.

Roderick, who trained as an architect, had been confronted with the possibilities of a life out of the rat race when working for the Centre for Alternative Technology in Wales; meanwhile Gillie had been building up a successful patchwork quilt and floor cushion business of her own. So the couple were well equipped to embark on a new life when they settled in Gloucestershire. 'People said we

were dropping out. We realized we were embarking on a new career,' they chorus.

The house they chose was, once again, a place in serious need of repair, a traditional stone Cotswold barn and a house that had been lived in by generations of bakers. The house itself was just habitable, but the barn had been destroyed in a fire caused by exploding flour dust. The Jameses' third son arrived shortly after building began, so the family had to prolong their stay in a rented house.

Roderick did the structural alterations himself. There was never any question of letting builders near the house. 'With a builder you can't afford to make all the little changes that make a house fun,' says Roderick, who is a firm believer that economically it makes better sense to give up work and do it yourself than slave away to pay for builders *and* support the family. Roderick's architectural training had given him some building experience; for her part, Gillie has always been a dab hand with a paintbrush. Between them they acquired all the other skills and did the lot – from plumbing to making their own furniture.

Their new home took as long to restore as the Welsh barn and was harder work: the existing interior of rotting units and rubbish had to be removed before they could start at all. Roderick's plan to insulate all the walls meant a complete rebuild of the inside. They moved the kitchen and bathroom, rewired, replumbed and converted the attic. Only when it came to the roof did they enlist outside help.

Time and trouble may be no object to Roderick and Gillie, but spending unnecessary money hurts. Their house is economically heated by open fires and heat from the kitchen stove, warmth being retained by the heavily insulated roof and walls (well disguised behind timber and rough plastered walls). 'We were dubious at first,' admits Roderick, 'and wondered whether we should have smooth plaster and fine joinery. In the end we decided this would be out of keeping with the architecture of the house'.

Over the years, the house has absorbed the Jameses' personal style. On the ground floor the flagstoned kitchen, full of colour and household clutter, and the quieter sitting room merge in a hallway that leads into a passage of busy workshops. Upstairs are several light, airy bedrooms, with the same sense of space as below; the attic contains spare rooms, Gillie's sewing room and a bathroom, which doubles as a darkroom.

PREVIOUS PAGE *A child-size gallery and balcony over the fireplace have been added at one end of the converted barn, a showcase of Roderick's skilful carpentry. Most of the furniture has been handmade from raw green oak, the two sofas are the only items that have been bought.*

LEFT *Handmade wooden units and masses of decorative plates give the kitchen a warm lived-in feel.*

ABOVE LEFT *A wooden
shorebird and heron
decorate the sitting
room.*

ABOVE RIGHT *A
collection of hand-
carved wooden birds
and boats against the
soft-pink plaster walls
of the barn.*

The result is simply furnished, but with fascinating and revealing details. Gillie supplies colour and pattern, Roderick texture and finish. But both disdain the notion of being perfectionists – 'we just like things to be visually pleasing'. For this reason, much has been left unfinished on purpose, such as rough saw marks on new door frames to match the older ones.

All the beds display Gillie's brilliant patch-works and collage cushions. Her fabric scenes of houses, people and flowers adorn various walls and every five years Gillie makes a commemorative collage of the family.

Although the interior belies it, nothing in the house is expensive. 'The Mexican tiles in the bathroom,' says Gillie, 'were the only luxury.' But the quest for perfection leads them quite far afield. Determined to find a large white bath rather than a small coloured one, for example, they tracked down a cast-iron 'reject' in Surrey that they transported on the car roof all the way back to the house in Gloucestershire.

Despite all their efforts and original touches, Gillie and Roderick decided the house was becoming a bit cramped, particularly after having lived in a barn. 'In a barn you're free to sculpt space, you can get away

and view people from different angles,' explains Roderick. Eventually they decided to restore their present barn. In it they would also house a new business: importing wooden model boats from an English craftsman living in Italy. Now the barn is their favourite part – a perfect space for both business and family life, with a movable partitioned office at one end for Roderick's consultancy and architec-tural work. The restoration is full of surprise and wit, with a child-size gallery and balcony over the fireplace, a curtained truckle bed hidden in one corner and a woven screen – all made with cheap green oak.

'Besides being far less expensive than seasoned oak, it bends slightly, has a more varied grain and is in keeping with the carpentry of a barn. But because it shrinks you have to work it in a different way.' The barn is a showcase for Roderick's skill with wood. There should be more art carpentry he believes. 'So much joinery is arid – finer but not as good.'

The decoration of the barn is peaceful and unimposing, with walls the soft pink the plasterer left them and curtains made by Gillie from striped Indian bedspreads. The windows are a small, but important feature: 'We don't want huge outward views that

make you feel gloomy on grey days.'

Of the furniture two enormous sofas are the only pieces they have bought. 'Everything else has been made by us or else handed down.' The long table which doubles as Roderick's desk was made from pine boards nailed on to an old feeding trough. A rush job, this – he needed it for a conference.

The same table is where they entertain, carrying food from the kitchen in between courses. They are not compulsively social but do enjoy dinner parties on special occasions. Fresh, additive-free food is preferred, but Gillie admits to 'doing everything with food as quickly as possible'. Largely self-sufficient, they also bake delicious bread, and there are home produced trout and duck from the pond. 'We do eat meat but also quite a lot of vegetarian food.' Who can blame them, as most of their vegetables and fruit are straight from the garden? This, too, required extensive work.

'It was a tip, full of rubbish, with hardly a flower in the place,' recalls Roderick. Now it is a child's paradise: a pleasing mixture of tamed garden and wilderness with a stream; a pond for all manner of aquatic diversions – canoes, coracles, water bicycles and trout; a treehouse, gypsy caravan and a five-acre woodland walk.

Gillie has planted climbers to creep over the Cotswold stone and she is just starting a flower garden. But her main preoccupation these days is with birds, and not the wild variety. A collector of decorative ducks and birds she has since made a business of her passion. Carved by Roderick, painted by Gillie, they are sold in the same galleries and shops as the boats. Having built up the venture into the profitable one it is today, they both find it incredibly satisfying, if time-consuming. 'We realize just how lucky we are being able to make money doing something we enjoy,' marvels Gillie who, like her husband, is loath to employ anyone else. 'We don't want to be a manufacturing company hacking out mass-produced birds,' stresses Roderick, 'even if we could make more money that way.'

The birds, which are hewn from huge planks of English lime, are based on nineteenth-century American decoys that were used on lakes and shores to lure flying birds to the hunter. Each bird is an original: hand-carved, sanded and painted to catch its spirit rather than every detail.

Besides their own birds, which sell for £45 upwards, Roderick and Gillie deal in work by other carvers and any original decoys they can find – those that Gillie can resist adding to her own collection, that is. The hardest part is selling – Gillie leaves that to Roderick – and a window display of birds last year suggests that he is clearly proficient. 'Shop-keepers can be so rude when you offer goods. I'm even sympathetic to Jehovah's Witnesses now!'

The business has become such an integral part of family life that even the boys can be found spending hours in the workshop, carving offcuts into primitive boats and birds. Where some fathers lay down port for their sons' coming of age, Roderick has laid down carpentry tools. The Jameses are very keen that the boys absorb their lifestyle. 'It's important to look at different ways of making a living. Instead of thinking you've got to go to an office, you can do just as well by being resourceful,' claims Roderick. 'I almost feel guilty making birds, thinking perhaps I should be doing "proper" work. But when you begin to make thousands of pounds, you realize it's perfectly proper work.'

It is not every couple who could live and work in this sort of proximity. But they make it work to their advantage, by continually discussing and criticizing what they make. Roderick was quite resigned on one occasion to taking a sledgehammer to a fireplace he had just finished when Gillie in her quiet assured way said it was too high . . .

Naturally, though, they both need a certain amount of space and time of their own. Gillie finds it principally in painting and making patchworks; Roderick's diversion, shared with his sons, is a 1936 gaff ketch, which he sails on the Solent when he can – and which he bought in very poor condition. 'It was hard work to restore, but in its former condition it cost half of what it's worth now.'

Holidays are thin on the ground for a couple who often put in seven days a week thirteen hours a day, with fifteen minutes for cheese on toast. 'Even when we do have a day off,' says Gillie, 'we're trying out new shapes and designs.' A 'Mrs Jenner' in Despatch is the only help they have with the business – and she is fictitious.

Even unassisted, life treats the Jameses well. 'We do live comfortably,' says Roderick, 'but we are careful with money. It is very worrying when we finish a contract if there are no more orders in sight. But proving that you can make a reasonable living with your hands is like having a pension – you know that you will always have a source of income to fall back on.'

The Jameses have established a successful business selling decorative wooden ducks and birds based on nineteenth-century American decoys. Hand-carved from English lime, each bird is painted individually by Gillie.

THROUGH EXPERT EYES

Joanna Laidlaw

Photographs by James Merrell

From a handsome Georgian mansion house near Cheltenham, John and Caroline Evetts organize the interior design of Landmark Trust properties throughout Britain.

The Landmark Trust is a peculiarly English set-up. It rescues buildings in distress. Anything industrial, ornamental, religious, or military: an old copper and arsenic mine; an Egyptian house; Fort Clonque on Alderney in the Channel Islands. But, not content with saving them from a crumbling death or certain destruction, it sets about making them into eccentric but sensible dwellings that are let to holiday-makers. The man responsible for furnishing and decorating these buildings, John Evetts, in true Landmark Trust style, is indisputably English, irrepressibly enthusiastic and has excellent taste. He lives with his wife Caroline in the additions of the eighteenth-century Hakewill-designed house where he was brought up. His parents live in the older part and the south front was left empty, save for the annual hunt ball, until recently. It has dauntingly large rooms which they have cunningly transformed to make a house that feels very young. What was once the dining room has been painted an unexpected and very pretty green. It is now part sitting room, part dining room, and part freestanding wooden kitchen (so as not to interfere with the architecture).

The south front of the superb Georgian mansion (TOP) *near Cheltenham where John and Caroline Evetts live; the stable block* (ABOVE)*; a corner of the workshop* (LEFT).

OPPOSITE *In the hall an alabaster bust, old prints and a collection of early Winchcombe pottery stand out against rosewood panelling.*

The imposing entrance hall is not often used and instead they have designed and built a much smaller hall at the side. This welcomes you into the house and up the stairs to the bedrooms which are gradually being redecorated. There is a formal drawing room with curtains designed by Sybil Colefax in 1947; Caroline and John have added wallpaper by Pugin. Here they entertain large groups who are touring country houses to tea or lunch. Caroline has been a professional cook for several years and does all the catering herself.

They have lived happily for several years above the very fine stables in which most of the Landmark Trust furniture is stored. It works well. The furniture is brought back from auction and divided up into houses and types and put into corresponding loose boxes. So if you are looking for a dining room chair, you can walk straight into the chair store and pick one from a forest of chairs stacked on top of each other and hanging from the ceiling and walls.

John Evetts has a tiny staff consisting of Les Haines who does the repairs, and Christine Lainé and Mary Hall, who are local magistrates living nearby; they come in twice a week to upholster. The entire staff of the Landmark Trust is small. It is headed by

John and Christian Smith who set up the Manifold Trust (forerunner of the Landmark Trust) in 1963 to try and save small or unusual properties. Each year some 10,000 people stay in about sixty wildly differing places, each looked after by local secretaries. Letting out the buildings for holidays involves the minimum of architectural changes, as short-term tenants do not need garages, outbuildings or gardens. It also ensures that the buildings are occupied almost all the time, not just by weekenders, and the income from the lets helps to finance each house.

RIGHT *The drawing room is the most formal room in the house with a gilt Regency chandelier and Queen Anne furniture; the curtains were designed by Sybil Colefax and the wallpaper is a design by Pugin.*

ABOVE RIGHT *The half-tester bed in the main bedroom was put together using a mixture of antique pieces.*

The task of furnishing is endless as once the first 'campers' (Landmark Trust jargon for a holiday-maker) have been installed, there then begins the enormous task of keeping abreast of repairs. Much of John's initial furnishing is designed to minimize this. Chairs have to have at least four stretchers for maximum strength; ratchets on arms and moving parts are made immovable to prevent breakage. 'You know the vagaries of your own furniture and you can tell people to be careful, but everything has to be camper-proof. Cabriole legs and Knole sofas are not made for people to bounce on, and tend simply to break. And anything uphol-stered has two sets of loose covers, so they can regularly be dry cleaned.'

Great care goes into selecting furniture that fits in with the look of the place. 'The important thing is that the furniture shouldn't jar or take away from the architec-ture of a place. If you walk into the room and the first thing you notice is the furniture and pictures, then I have done my job badly.' It is a sort of anonymous, gentleman's-club style of decorating.

John does not go to many local sales ('too expensive'), and most of the pieces are bought from local traders, many of whom now come directly to him. He is looking for very specific

things 'I actually prefer my furniture to be not quite right so I can afford it.' He is, however, uncompromising about how it should look. Most of the pieces are nineteenth century, and nearly all the upholstery is Edwardian, but there is more to it than that. Single chairs, for example, represent very good value at the moment: a single Hepple-white chair costs around £50. 'A complete set of chairs is no good, for as soon as a camper has broken it you lose not just the value of the chair but also the set.' All Landmark pro-perties are therefore furnished with harlequin sets of like-looking chairs. On the other hand, old joint stools and whatnots are prohibi-tively expensive to buy and it costs far less to have them made by a local craftsman.

Once a house is furnished, the job goes on. John carries around with him a mental image of a space between two windows in one house, or the oval panelling in another, until he finds exactly the object or picture that he is looking for. A trip to the local town to buy cheese also produces a plaster Egyptian obelisk, nine inches high, perfect for the Egyptian house in Penzance. Often the most unpredictable fur-niture or pictures are used. 'What is impor-tant is the sense of humour of it all. I sometimes put in things that are irrelevant, and sometimes irreverent.' It works.

LEFT *Upholsterers Mary Hall and Christine Lainé and repair man Les Haines at work in the main workshop, formerly the old kitchen.*

OPPOSITE *John Evetts in the old larder, now a picture-framing workshop.*

PARTNERS IN WIT

Suzanne Askham

Photographs by
Alistair Morrison

The home of writers Terence Brady and Charlotte Bingham stretches out between trees in gently rolling Somerset countryside and looks deceptively sleepy. Honeysuckle and roses clamber up walls of fudge-coloured stone, creating a picture that cannot have changed dramatically in two hundred years.

But then as I approach, the front door is hurled open by a half-grown, heavy-pawed bearded collie, and the air of drowsiness promptly vanishes. One dog is followed by another, a snooty nosed little Lhasa apso, and bringing up the rear are their owners, Charlotte Bingham and Terence Brady. As they guide me into the house with promises of tea, I am reminded of amiable P. G. Wodehouse characters.

The husband and wife writing team has produced such television classics as *No, Honestly, Pig in the Middle* and *Nanny*, as well as episodes of *Upstairs, Downstairs*. In addition, Charlotte has written a string of novels about muddled up aristocrats while Terence continues to write prodigiously for papers and magazines. They have also recently completed a film for television, and a play called *I Wish, I Wish*, about a woman who wishes herself back to being nineteen again.

When not actually writing they go horse-riding or racing. It is a grand passion; Terence is a trainer *manqué*. 'I'm embarrassed to admit how many horses we have,' says Terence. 'There are two showjumpers and a racehorse at home and two racehorses in

Salisbury being trained by a marvellous friend of ours, Peter Bailey.'

Eight years ago the Bradys lived in Richmond with scarcely a thought of the country. 'We were caught in that awful education trap, reluctant to take our children away from good local schools,' explains Terence 'And Charlotte was an absolute townie. She used to hold the view that the country was where your husband sent you if you'd been unfaithful.'

When they finally decided to make a move, their children Candida and Matthew proved ungratefully willing to go. Finding a suitable house took four more years until Terence's sister found this. 'It was perfect,' he says. 'It's the sort of house Englishmen dream of when they're abroad. We told the lady selling it we'd have it and she actually fell into the cabbages with surprise.'

Appalling things happened during their first summer. One day a helicopter sprayed the surrounding fields and the whole garden died. 'We went outside the next morning and it was as though we'd suffered nuclear fall-out.' Fortunately, with advice from Alan Eason, chief gardener at nearby Hadspen House, and with continuing help from his assistant Jerry Bird, today it all looks almost as good as it did.

Then there was the problem with the stove. 'We didn't have one. Terence said we could cook on an open fire. He put the casserole on and it exploded up the chimney. Then the chimney itself caught fire. We decided it is obviously more difficult living in the old ways than one might think.'

Troubles afflicting the Bradys are invariably put to good use. Over the last few months they have been writing up their past predicaments in a television drama, *A View of Meadows Green*.

Their mellow-stoned home has escaped more or less unscathed from the early disasters. In redecorating they have followed the principle of trying not to disturb too much. The previous owner had painted and papered the walls in warm pastel shades, which the Bradys have kept, simply adding the occasional border 'from one of those posh wallpaper places'. Some of the furniture came from Richmond; other pieces have been bought from local dealers – in particular, from Ron Greenman, a furniture restorer in Bath. An elderly grand piano in the drawing room was acquired only when the man selling it had satisfied himself it was going to a good home. In the kitchen, a dresser, probably as

old as the house, has been painted sky blue and joined by rows of blue shelves made up especially by a local carpenter.

The overall effect is remarkably pleasant, as neat and restful as one of Jane Austen's houses. Outside, the garden looks like a series of rooms, too: a big walled one full of cultivated shrubs; then a wild one scattered with snowdrops in spring; and then a watery one where an outdoor swimming pool slumbers till the summer.

The Brady day starts at eight o'clock or thereabouts in the kitchen, with breakfast in front of a huge warming log fire. Nowadays it is often just the two of them, as Matthew is at a weekly boarding school and Candida is away earning herself an Equity card. Mae, Matthew's cockatiel (a miniature version of a cockatoo) surveys Terence and Charlotte from a high perch and shrieks companionably from time to time. Later in the day, she will fly up to Charlotte's study and rush around demonically while Charlotte works. Charlotte and Terence have separate studies. Terence's is a comfortable affair stuffed with books and an indispensable word-processor. Charlotte's looks surprisingly like a bedroom, complete with a bed on which she likes to think up the next turn of a plot.

When they are working on a situation comedy the Bradys write together. 'It was dreadfully embarrassing when we first tried it,' remembers Charlotte. 'The silences were worse than anything. But it's a very good way of getting to know someone. You get

PREVIOUS PAGE *Terence Brady and Charlotte Bingham in the drawing room of their Somerset home.*

ABOVE FROM LEFT TO RIGHT *Horseriding and racing are two of the Bradys' favourite pastimes; a cockatiel keeps a watchful eye over Charlotte and cat, Maud, from the kitchen dresser; the garden at the back of the house is, like much of their land, kept wild.*

RIGHT *The colour scheme in the dining room remains much as it was when the Bradys moved in; a collection of rosettes* (RIGHT BELOW) *won at various events around the country decorates the cloakroom.*

writing partnerships in comedy more than anything else – I think because it's so difficult. Humour is such an idiosyncratic thing; it's almost impossible to tell what people will find funny.'

When it comes to the romantic scenes Charlotte's highly developed sense of humour lets her down. She has to give up entirely, and leave Terence to stand, as it were, in the place of both hero and heroine, because they have discovered he is more convincing about it than she is. This is no doubt partly due to the remarkable fact that he can turn his hand to almost anything, music and painting and acting included (he has appeared in the West End and in his own series). It has been said that Terence has the professional skill, while Charlotte has the comic genius.

One of the nicest things that has struck them since moving out to Somerset is how easy it is to make friends. 'We thought we'd have to import them but you don't. We knew some people already: painters and people in the business; and the horses are a contact. Terry does some eventing and showjumping, and we regularly go to Wincanton racecourse, which is just a couple of miles away. We hate the dinner party circuit though; they tried to get us into it but Terry has a very good way of refusing things. He says, "I'm terribly sorry, but we don't do that sort of thing".'

Instead the Bradys specialize in lunch parties, sharing the cooking, though Terry tends to create the exotic Indian, Indonesian and oriental dishes. 'The only time he gets temperamental is in the kitchen,' says Charlotte darkly.

But much of their time is spent simply exploring the countryside, riding over the local Downs and through the nearby Stourhead estate. 'You can see a lot more of the countryside on horseback. We know a field full of rare wild flowers which you can only get to by horse.'

They retain a refreshing interest in everything they see. 'In some farms, time hasn't moved since the thirteenth century,' says Charlotte with awe in her voice. 'There's sacking in the windows, sheep in the kitchen, and even in the living room at times.' Terence continues: 'Many of the attitudes are ancient, too. They won't give you grazing unless they want something from you . . . it's a real barter system.'

And as the Bradys consider their strange neighbours you can imagine, deep inside their writers' brains, new plots hatching for a future drama.

BETWEEN THE WAUGHS

Sylvia Howe

Photographs by Alistair Morrison

Auberon Waugh and his wife Lady Teresa live in the rambling seventeenth-century house in Somerset that his parents owned before him. The son of Evelyn Waugh is married to the daughter of the sixth Earl of Onslow and both share a consuming passion for food, wine and words.

Auberon took over the editorship of *The Literary Review* in 1986, his wife, a former cookery columnist, is the author of *Painting Water* and *Waterloo, Waterloo* and together they have recently produced a book of recipes with wines to complement them. The recipes are by Lady Teresa, the wine advice by Auberon. 'By no means a nitwit's guide,' he says. 'It assumes nothing more really about the readers than a desire to have good wine, but I jolly well expect them to know the difference between a burgundy and a claret.' The book sprang from their shared enjoyment of playing host together at Combe Florey.

His experience of wine and its consumption, we agree, equipped him outstandingly for the task. An already pink complexion deepens a little with pleasure. 'Yes, I admit that I've drunk extensively.'

The couple have no further plans for books. 'It's a one-off kind of thing. Really a bit of a pot-boiler,' he giggles in hesitant baritone, clearly and unashamedly enjoying his own joke.

Waugh is not at all as I imagined him – the cantankerous right-winger of the *Private Eye* Diaries, the grumpy son of a famously choleric father. He is a perfectly charming, rather puckish man, sporting the most spectacular pair of bright blue paisley braces imaginable over a neat, conservatively striped shirt. This is entertainment.

I am late, but he makes it instantly seem that to him another hour, or four, would be entirely acceptable. Hovering endearingly over his manuscript, he expands on his favourite topic: 'We have a huge cellar at Combe Florey. Nine cellars, actually, underneath the house, of which four are now full. My life's ambition is to fill all nine before I retire, which will be whenever I stop paying for my children. Then I can just sit back and drink my way through it.'

Waugh's main output (apart from what he calls his 'non-books' – that is, collections of his writings) is journalistic. 'I do a weekly thing in *The Spectator*, and a weekly thing at the moment for the *Daily Mail*, although that's going to change to either the *Daily Telegraph* or *The Independent*. It's just a weekly book review. I do wine in *Harpers Queen* (*sic*) and run *The Spectator* wine club. Then there's a fortnightly piece in the *Sunday Telegraph*. No, no novels at all, but I hope when I retire, I'll write a collection of drivelling novels. It's good to have a life plan!'

It is not surprising, with all this going on, that when he is at Combe Florey, Auberon

OPPOSITE *Auberon and Lady Teresa Waugh in their picturesque garden at Combe Florey in Somerset.*

RIGHT *The stable courtyard provides a colourful display of flowers in pots.*

eschews the delights of the tennis court, croquet lawns and boating lake in favour of reading quietly in the garden. He has the knack of making the most ordinary comment in the manner of one imparting a great revelation – a useful tactic, because it stops interviewers going off the beaten track.

By contrast, Teresa Waugh's manner is brisk, so brisk that few would dare to wander uninvited off the subject. She is straightforward and efficient, and her character

ABOVE *A long winding drive up to Combe Florey passes a little lake.*

OPPOSITE *One of Auberon Waugh's many writing commitments is a wine column for* The Spectator; *there are nine cellars underneath the house.*

seems to be reflected in the house, in which the only clutter is books and wine.

Lady Teresa speaks warmly of Combe Florey, which Evelyn Waugh bought in 1956. His wife stayed on until 1972, before moving into a wing to make way for the younger generation. 'There's an extremely beautiful Elizabethan gatehouse built, I think, in 1595, and there was originally an Elizabethan house which formed a courtyard with a gatehouse, burnt down at some stage. Our house is on the top of a hill, so it's further back from where the original house would have

been – and this was built at the end of the seventeenth century. It was added to, and has an eighteenth-century front and not very nice windows. Unfortunately, someone changed the frames.

'We've done away with what used to be the kitchen and made the old dining room into a kitchen. Although we do have a room which is sometimes used as a dining room, we usually eat in the kitchen: that's the only basic change.'

It is in the kitchen that Lady Teresa spends much of her time. But she is far from being a fanatical hostess. 'I don't like the word entertaining. It seems to me to conjure up something totally false.' But that does not mean she does not try at all: 'I cook an awful lot because I have a large family and a large number of relations who live round about, and quite a few friends who come from time to time. I see my cooking as cooking for whoever happens to be here.'

Auberon echoes Lady Teresa's feelings: 'Entertaining is limited only by my poor wife's readiness to cook. It's a hell of a lot of work if you've got a big house party, providing them with three meals a day.'

Although her main occupation is writing, Lady Teresa has done some translating – she was awarded a First in French and Italian at Exeter in her late thirties. Her views about writing are as firm as they are about cooking: 'It's no good just waiting for the mood to strike you, or else you'd never do it. I usually decide that I need a fairly free week and I am going to work three days. Then I work those mornings, setting myself a definite amount. I love putting ink on to paper. I love the actual physical process of writing. Why don't others say that? Why do they all write on typewriters?'

Perhaps because their scrawl is illegible.

Ink on paper or dishes on the table, both are accomplishments of the Waughs, and the combination of skills is clearly a thoroughly successful one.

CASA COLONICA
Mathew Spender
Photographs by Timothy Beddow

Most of the houses of Chianti have been built since the middle of the eighteenth century – giving the region its architectural unity. Many older monuments still exist, of course, seething with the memory of ancient and bloody events. Frederick Barbarossa was wounded by an arrow in the siege of Monteluco, within sight to the north from our back garden. To the south lies the River Arbia, which Dante described as having run red with the blood of Sienese and Florentines, killed in some horrible twelfth-century frontier dispute. On the horizon are the remains of an Etruscan town, sacked by the troops of Marius or perhaps of Sulla.

Perhaps some air of the untameable still clung to the land in the eighteenth century, when the archduke in Florence made it advantageous – tax-deductible – to invest in a new agricultural estate in the Chianti hills. Most of the *case coloniche* date from that time: *colonica* means belonging to the new peasant farmers, the colonists of the wild. The deal meant sharing agricultural produce, in return for the use of a new house and its surrounding land. The fields themselves were to be carved by hand from the neighbouring woods; each family would make perhaps one terrace per year, as arranged with the *fattore*, or owner's bailiff. It is unclear to me whether the deal could ever have been advantageous to either side. The owners, paid in kind, seldom had

enough capital to reinvest in terms of new equipment, care of the houses and so forth. Few aristocratic owners could be bothered to sell their myriad wares intelligently and, as a result, the people who profited were the *fattori*, whose skill in cheating both sides was a source of respectful wonder to all concerned. For the most part, the one idea of the owners was to shell out as little hard cash as possible. This meant that the peasants had to become virtually self-sufficient. Even the seeds for next year's crop had to be their own, which was reflected naturally in the ensuing crop. Thus the owners received as rent some bushels of imperfect barley, wine from here, there and everywhere – some good, some bad – and olive oil, the market for which was, and still tends to be, strictly local.

When we first came here in 1968, we saw the tail end of a system that had brought little profit to either side. My nearest neighbour earned, so he told me, a total annual income of some £85, from the sale of his half of an ox. But then he only needed cash for cigarettes and bus tickets, and as he smoked little and never went anywhere, he was quite content.

One fine relic of this time-honoured arrangement is that the houses in the area have a strong architectural consistency. Evidently the archduke sent out architects to supervise the initial spate of building. Later, the peasants perforce made their own improvements, but the agricultural priorities and the strong

PREVIOUS PAGE *The Tuscan home where artist Mathew Spender lives with his wife Maro and their two daughters.*

LEFT *Mathew, son of poet Stephen Spender, in his studio.*

BELOW *The Tuscan farmhouse kitchen; the study bedroom.*

OPPOSITE *Maro, also a painter, decorated the dining table herself.*

local building tradition ensured that the changes have their own natural, organic sense of architectural style. Our own house is a simple *casa colonica*, its charm coming from the central tower: in its peasant days pigeons were housed there and bred for the table, now it contains one of our delightful daughters.

The *mezadria*, or share-cropping arrangement, died in the Sixties, when the peasants either changed jobs and moved to the cities or became agricultural wage earners, moving out of the *case coloniche* to go into council houses. The owners sold the abandoned houses either to foreigners like us, or to rich city dwellers who wanted a place in the country. This has resulted in a certain cultural trauma. The stalls and rusting farm equipment have been replaced by nice new tiles, central heating and carpets on the floor. To my mind the spirit of these houses has in some cases been destroyed, mainly where the style of the new inhabitants is too remote from that of the old.

I hope this is not the case for us. But painters and sculptors are manually occupied in a way that is not so different from the life of peasants, and professionally we address as colleagues the local masons, carpenters and potters with whom we often work. Three or four times a year we all congregate in the local band, where I stand, fourth on the left, among some young clarinettists half my height. Our life is the diametrical opposite,

LEFT *The bathroom, which was originally a bedroom, houses a porcelain bath from a monks' seminary.*

BELOW *The courtyard garden is full of terracotta pots brimming with greenery.*

ABOVE *Individually glazed pigeonholes in the guest bedroom in the tower.*

one might say, of such casual migrants as Lord Lambton, who feuds with his neighbours from five hills away and is so poorly assimilated into his surroundings that he deems it necessary to call the place 'Chiantishire'.

A life to be recommended? Yes, if your job can take it. Excellent for production, but lousy for distribution, for which you have to go to the big city like everybody else. Very good for marriage, which these days has to be cultivated like some rare prehensile cactus. Wonderful for bringing up children. Our own, now fourteen and sixteen, have decided they are Italian, but the moment of mental panic this involved was mine, not theirs.

Retreat from the city to the country entails no real escape from the cerebral baggage one has already accumulated, though it certainly gives a chance of getting it into some sort of order. In that sense, whatever the beauty of our surroundings, and the effort we expend in making it more beautiful, the world is not as real as how you reconstruct it, just as the earth, as the Etruscans believed, is no more than a transient reflection of the sky.

WRITING IN THE FAMILY

Charles Darwent

Photographs by Alistair Morrison

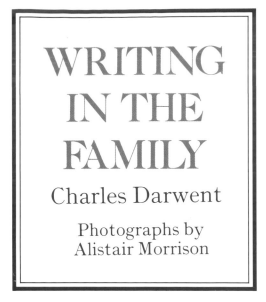

The problem for the would-be literary sleuth lies in the sheer breadth of Lady Rachel Billington's writing. Consider her heroines: some, like their creator, are well-bred, soignée and live in country houses. Near the mark, in fact: the Billington family lives in the oldest continuously inhabited house in Dorset. It is a honey-coloured Ham stone manor, with trefoil windows, stone-flagged floors and a court room where assizes – like the one that condemned Thomas Hardy's Tess – were held. But then again some of her heroines are working class, frumpy, and come from East Acton (or Ireland, or Venice, or New York). They may, like their creator, be happily married – or they may not. And as if this chameleon quality of her heroines does not make Rachel Billington elusive enough, the befuddled investigator must also cope with the following fact: the protagonists of three of her nine novels (including the latest, *The Garish Day*) are *men*.

'I often identify more with men than with women,' says Lady Rachel, with a half smile, at once reserved and full of amused complicity. She is a beautiful woman, exquisite in a fine Renaissance way, and this identification with the opposite sex seems faintly incongruous. 'I grew up with lots of brothers,' she continues (she is one of the Pakenham family), 'and it never occurred to us that we should be treated differently from each other.'

What Rachel Billington means by 'identifying with men' is that she resents the categorization of women – and especially of women who write – as something different. 'I mean, who ever heard of "men writers"?' she questions. 'Women writers', on the other hand, apparently form, in the (male-dominated) critical eye, an amorphous crew including everyone from Mrs Gaskell to Jackie Collins. 'When people – women included – hear that you are writing,' she continues, 'they assume that it's simply a hobby to fill in time between doing the washing-up and doing the ironing. It couldn't possibly be a profession.'

Rachel Billington's impatience with this attitude has increased over the years. For instance, her feeling towards that doyenne of 'women writers', Jane Austen. Five years ago, Lady Rachel said that Austen 'may not have been entirely at a disadvantage' in having had to accept a passive role in life (the cause, perhaps, of her 'seeing eye'). Now she finds it almost impossible to read *Pride and Prejudice* without a growing sense of anger at its authoress's passivity. 'Jane Austen was a voyeur,' she says. 'She doesn't get involved, and so she can afford to be very, very critical. That's not for me at all.' Not for her, either, the sink-bound heroines of Margaret Drabble or the wounded fragility of Anita Brookner (both writers, though, whose talent Lady Rachel admires): whatever the apparent differences between Billington heroines, they are all mistresses of their own destiny. It is this quality which underlies her love for Hardy's novels, and which, in turn, 'has a lot to do,' she says. 'with my love for Dorset ... with its space and sweeping views, and its intimate, little areas.'

Lest all this sound as though Lady Rachel is what she calls 'a battling feminist', let me point out that nothing could be further from the truth. Her house is full of children (she and film-maker husband Kevin Billington have two boys and two girls, between the ages of six and sixteen). Chairs come from an old officers' mess, the Billingtons spend most of their time in the kitchen, and the house has not been redecorated since they bought it; decorations tend to be indestructible or out of reach, the old Japanese horse blanket above the drawing room window is both. With its mixture of precious paintings and kindergarten collage, the Billington house is clearly a home. Caspar, the younger son, marches into the drawing room, fixes his mother's interviewer with frank, brown eyes, and says mysteriously, 'I've learnt to ride my bicycle.' The scene is most un-Brooknerish.

PREVIOUS PAGE *Built of honey-coloured stone, the Billingtons' home is the oldest continuously inhabited house in Dorset.*

ABOVE *The Billington family and friends at the dining table.*

OPPOSITE *Immediately next to the house is the lovely village church.*

ABOVE *The large family kitchen, like the rest of the house, has not been decorated since the Billingtons moved in.*

LEFT *The Dorset countryside stretches out all around the house providing the Billington family with many interesting walks.*

At the same time, Rachel Billington has every sympathy with the plight of her fellow authoresses. 'Did you notice that *not one* of the four female Booker Prize finalists in 1985 was a mother?' she asks. I had not. She smiles: 'You see, there's an essential problem, in that motherhood takes out of a woman exactly the same emotions as novel writing. Men expend their energies in different ways, and so it's easier for them.'

Ah, but is she not a Pakenham woman? And is this breed not famed for its fecundity in motherhood as in authorship? Lady Longford had eight children, and still found time to turn out respected biographies of Wellington and Queen Victoria; Rachel's sister Lady Antonia Pinter has six, and four biographies (and several novels) under her belt; and although niece Flora has no children yet, she too burst into print recently. How can one family bring so much into the world?

'You see,' says Lady Rachel, 'my mother didn't really begin to write until we were relatively old, nor did my sister Antonia until her children were older too. We didn't grow up in a literary atmosphere at all. I just got used to writing before all my children grew up.' The accepted wisdom is that Pakenhams simply inherit writing in the way that other children inherit noses; but Rachel Billington would contest this view. She declares that, if anything, the influence of her husband was more important as a literary catalyst – favourite episodes in the Billington autobiography are that Lady Rachel began her first novel while snowed up on their Scottish honeymoon, and that Kevin Billington used to lock her in her room while she wrote (the habit has obviously stuck: she still does most of her writing in the four-poster bed which they bought in Sherborne). But all of these are red herrings. To the question of *why* Rachel Billington writes, the simple answer is because she wants to.

And where does Lady Rachel Billington see her place in the pantheon of English fiction? 'Fiction in this country,' she says acidly, 'is not seen as a scholarly occupation. On the review pages of any newspaper or magazine, by far the greater space is given over to factual works. In the United States they don't make this distinction between "serious" and "popular" writers.'

In her own works, she tries to dispel the myth of there being two types of fiction: Billington stories are written to entertain. They may *also* instruct (*The Big Dipper*, for instance, carries an unmistakable warning about modern permissiveness), but only in passing – it will not have been written didactically. 'I suppose I want my books to be seen as comedies of manners,' says Lady Rachel. 'If you were to ask me to name the modern English writer I most admire, then it would have to be Iris Murdoch. One couldn't say that she was comic' (she smiles quickly) 'although her books have a certain lugubrious humour. And she certainly has "meaning".'

Interestingly, her latest novel *The Garish Day* moves nearer to an exploration of Roman Catholicism: its title is taken from Cardinal Newman's hymn, 'Lead Kindly Light', and the book has been promoted in America as a Catholic work – although, stresses its writer, that was not how she had intended it. 'I have noticed the Church creeping into my recent books, but it isn't intentional.' She pauses, thoughtfully. Her parents are devout Catholic laymen, and she herself feels that Catholicism provides 'a structure for a good life'. Then she adds, with humour, 'Whether or not we can live up to it is another matter again. It's like squirming on a hook: I do a lot of squirming.'

True to the woman and her work, however, this momentary confession is followed by an irreverent anecdote about the Pakenhams at prayer. Her father, a fine example of the belief that converts are always the most zealous practitioners (for example Malcolm Muggeridge, who was converted by Lord Longford and returned the compliment by introducing Rachel Pakenham to her husband), tried to institute evening family prayers. 'It was,' says Lady Rachel, 'a disaster. My father used to kneel in a *very* holy way, and my sister and I would get the giggles. Fortunately, it didn't last very long.'

For the future, Rachel Billington will be spending a lot of time in that Dorset four-poster bed. She has been commissioned to do a serial for television and she is also working on another novel, to be called *Loving Attitudes*. It is unlikely to deal overtly with questions of existentialist angst, or the depression of female university lecturers, and as a result her detractors – who often do confine themselves to these subjects – will continue to dismiss her as slight. Rachel Billington clearly could not care less: her intention is not to preach, but to discuss universal questions in a straightforward, human and often light-hearted way.

'I have,' says Lady Rachel Billington, 'a rather optimistic view of people and of the world.'

AT HOME WITH JEFFREY ARCHER

Linda Franklin

Photographs by Martyn Goddard

The church clock might have stood at 'ten to three' in Rupert Brooke's day, but this would not do for Jeffrey Archer. Today's favourite son of Grantchester appreciates punctuality and beams when we arrive a minute early. For several years, the Archers have lived in The Old Vicarage, Grantchester, after which the famous poem is named, with their sons William and James. Mary Archer, Jeffrey's wife, teaches chemistry at Cambridge University near by. Their listed seventeenth-century house squats behind a red-brick wall just off the main road through the village, in grounds that stretch down to the River Cam.

Jeffrey Archer is still on top form. The consistently bestselling author has been married for over twenty years to Mary, who is both extremely clever and very nice.

Jeffrey went to Oxford, ran for Great Britain in the 1964 Olympics and was elected to the Greater London Council at the age of twenty-six. In 1969, he became the youngest Member of Parliament when he won the Conservative seat of Louth in Lincolnshire. He was a rising star, tipped to go far. Then came the unforeseen crash. In 1974, a Canadian company in which he had invested heavily, collapsed dismally, leaving him nearly half a million pounds in debt.

He resigned from the House and started again from scratch. His first novel, *Not a Penny More, Not a Penny Less*, was an instant

success; since then, he has published six more novels and has made a lot of money. Just as he could well afford to take a sabbatical from writing to indulge his love of politics, he could well afford to renovate his Grantchester home when he bought it in 1979.

Before the Archers took it over, the house had belonged to the Ward family. On Rupert Brooke's death in 1915, the poet's mother bought the house he had loved and presented it to his close friend, Dudley Ward. When he died, it passed to Dudley's son, Peter, in whose hands it remained until the Archers bought it. The family did not move in until the summer of 1980, after most of the necessary work had been done – damp courses, central heating, rewiring. Mary designed it all; Jeffrey claims he knew nothing about it. The Wards had divided the house into two in order to take in lodgers, so the Archers' first task was to make it a family house again. This done, the kitchen received attention: it had looked like the engine room of the *Queen Mary*. It became one large kitchen and breakfast room, and was made to look less institutional by moving a door from the end to the side. The old Aga, sadly, had to go (no place to put it where the flue would not be a problem) and Mary had a traditional-style oven by Bulthaup installed. 'Gleaming High Tech would have been out of place here,' she explains, 'so I decided to go for something that is fairly conventional and countrified. Much the same applies to the rest of the house, which really suggested its own brief,' says Mary. 'It's old and homely – a comfortable, medium-sized house of timber and brick. There are lovely old walls and no right angles ... With that you're limited in decoration style. I went for something not exactly cottagey, but then again, not grand – really, I tried to aim for prettiness above all else.'

Thus the style is mellow, the walls gently colour-washed, the timber exposed, the antique furniture hospitably well worn. The dining room has a large, stained oak dining table with matching carved oak chairs, gleaming quarry tiles on the floor and braided and embroidered curtains. In the sitting room is a piano, which Mary plays, in velvet and chintz surroundings – a far cry from the boys' quarters where a computer and a music system reign.

Jeffrey Archer loves contrast and travelling, but at the end of every hectic trip to America to promote his books, he is always happy to return to his rural retreat in Grantchester.

PREVIOUS PAGE
Bestselling author Jeffrey Archer in the grounds of his historic Grantchester home. In 1969, aged 26, he became the youngest Member of Parliament when he won the Conservative seat of Louth in Lincolnshire.

LEFT FROM THE TOP
Mary Archer at the piano in the sitting room of The Old Vicarage; the grounds of the listed seventeenth-century house stretch down to the River Cam; the dining room has a large, stained oak table with matching chairs on a quarry-tiled floor.

OPPOSITE *The walls are colour-washed and original timbers exposed to retain the character of the lovely old house.*

A NICE LINE
IN LAUGHTER

Joanna Laidlaw

Photographs by Alistair Morrison

A few years ago author and journalist Jilly Cooper and her family moved from Putney to Gloucestershire. Arriving at their house is rather like stepping straight into one of her novels. Set in a classic Gloucestershire village, there are children, animals, noise, commotion and, in the distance, a dog drinking out of the lavatory pan.

You are ushered in by her secretary Annalise and clucked over and made to feel very welcome, for Jilly Cooper is indisputably nice. She is also very clever. *Riders*, her 350,000-word blockbuster about showjumping, shot to the number one bestseller slot and is being made into a film. But it is her knack of pinpointing esoteric English habits and writing about them wickedly and wittily that has made her famous.

It was only quite recently that Jilly moved to the country to join the 'nouveau ruralists'. 'My mother always had fantasies about me in the country with gumboots, but it just seemed too Utopian. I have to be where the action is, to fight the battle between stimulation and serenity,' says Jilly. However, Putney lost its attractions over the years – 'too many rapes and too much like a goldfish bowl. Every weekend crowds of people would spend the whole time drinking our drink and we would achieve nothing'. Much to the disgust of their teenage children, Felix and Emily, they decided to move.

They found the house quickly; somebody told them about it while they were on a Great Paw trek at Longleat. It is very pretty. Made of mellow Cotswold stone, it lies on the edge of a village looking down the length of a valley. Built in the thirteenth century, it was designed as a chantry house for monks (a chapel for the chanting of masses for the dead); in the 1830s two more neo-Perpendicular wings were added and it is in one of these that Jilly has her study and she and Leo their bedroom. So far, the house has been left much as it was when they bought it. But they have decorated it with a multitude of pictures and put a jukebox in the cloakroom.

The front door opens on to a stone-flagged hall with an elegant staircase well. The whole of this and the landing is painted a rather surprising shade of pink, which they inherited from the previous owner, Suna Boyle, a society beauty. It looks rather good as a backdrop for their hotchpotch of paintings, including many portraits and dog pictures. A green baize door (put in as a joke) goes through to an unpretentious kitchen with a pretty windowseat under a mullioned window. This is where you are likely to find dogs, cats and children.

Leo is much the better cook and it is he who puts together the big family meals, leaving them to survive on eggs and salads when he goes to London in the middle of the week.

ABOVE *The Cooper family on the terrace.*

OPPOSITE FROM THE TOP *The book-lined winter sitting room; Leo Cooper's neat military-inspired study in the oldest part of the house; Jilly with her secretary in the kitchen.*

PREVIOUS PAGE *The mellow Cotswold stone home of author Jilly Cooper and her family was built in the thirteenth century as a chantry house for monks.*

The family alternates between two sitting rooms downstairs; a cool and rather elegant summer one which opens on to the terrace, and a cosier wintry one in which Jilly sometimes plays the piano.

Leo has his study in the oldest and coldest part of the house; it is also uncarpeted – 'a fantastic dance floor'. He started his own military publishing company in 1969, and his writing efforts have been limited to a few 'silly' books with Jilly on sport. 'I don't really like writing,' he says, 'and I see what a hard slog it is.'

Jilly's study is the complete opposite of Leo's. Painted a mysterious shade of mauve (also inherited from Suna) and overlooking the valley, it is where Jilly works every day; she describes herself as 'quite professional but not efficient. When despair, the bank manager or the debtors' prison looms, then I do something about it'.

Her family seems quite used to her working to tight deadlines, and she ignores everything when she has something to finish, often sitting up all night, 'making that obtrusive, miserable sound of somebody who can't get a piece together'. She writes all her books in longhand, in handwriting so bad that it would be better suited to a doctor's prescription pad, and her secretary types them out into something legible.

The planning begins with the characters, each of whom is allotted four pages in a large notebook; these are built up until a plot emerges. Family and friends are called upon to give advice, and you feel some of the things you say are being filed away to be used as a fictitious character trait later on. The final synopsis may not be very long; the advance for *Riders* was raised on a mere four pages. *Riders* did, however, take a very long time to reach publication. It was originally finished in 1972, when Jilly went out to lunch, got drunk and left the manuscript either in a taxi or on a beauty counter in a department store. She did not finish the rewriting for twelve years.

Jilly gets very involved with each book – 'like sex, you get very dependent in the hope that it's good' – and she is a perfectionist, sometimes doing fifteen drafts until she gets it right. Leo acts as a very good sounding board, endlessly patient.

'He is married to authors all day at the office, then comes home to me and puts up with my misery, angst and agony.' The two of them seem enviably happy due, perhaps, to Jilly's secret formula for a successful mar-

RIGHT *The pink landing; the colour was inherited from a previous owner.*

OPPOSITE *The house lies on the edge of a village with a view down the length of a valley.*

Jilly in her study.

riage – 'creaking bedsprings from sex and giggling after parties'.

The whole set-up is tantalizingly normal. Jilly spends much of her time in the country, going to London infrequently. When she does go she puts off washing her hair until the last possible moment as 'the dogs know I am going to London as soon as they see the shampoo'.

Felix and Emily are also at home during the holidays. Felix is sporting a haircut that is 'a cross between a lavatory brush and a hedgehog' and the glamorous Emily is emerging from a smoke-filled bedroom pasted with black and white pin-ups. Both seem completely unperturbed by their mother's success. And so is she.

ACKNOWLEDGEMENTS

The publishers and *Country Homes and Interiors* are most grateful to the owners of all the houses and gardens featured, without whose forbearance neither this book nor the magazine could have been produced. The publishers would also like to extend their thanks to World Press Network and all the photographers who kindly supplied material for reproduction.

Copyright © Carlton Magazines 1987

First published in Great Britain in 1987
by George Weidenfeld & Nicolson Ltd

First published in the United States by Salem House Publishers, 1987
462 Boston Street, Topsfield, MA 01983

Library of Congress Cataloging-in-Publication Data

The English country home.

Compilation of articles published in Country
homes and interiors.
Includes index.
1. Country homes—England. 2. Country life—
England. 3. England—Social life and customs—
20th century. 4. Interior decoration—England.
5. Gardens—England. I. Berridge, Vanessa, 1955–
DA660.E54   1987   728′.0942   86-31309
ISBN 0-88162-239-7

Designed by Joy FitzSimmons
Filmset by Keyspools Ltd
Printed and bound in Italy

The publishers are grateful to
St Martin's Press, Inc., New York, for permission to reproduce an
extract from *James Herriot's Yorkshire* on pages 138–41
(Copyright © Text 1979 by James Herriot;
Copyright © Photographs by Michael Joseph Ltd).